What Time is it There?

For Line
For Jean-Michel

— **What Time** — **is it There?**

America and Islam at the Dawn of Modern Times

— Serge Gruzinski —

Translated by Jean Birrell

polity

First published in French as *Quelle heure est-il là-bas?* © Editions du Seuil, 2008

This English edition © Polity Press, 2010

Ouvrage publié avec le concours du Ministère français de la Culture – Centre national du livre

Published with the assistance of the French Ministry of Culture – National Centre for the Book

Polity Press
65 Bridge Street
Cambridge CB2 1UR, UK

Polity Press
350 Main Street
Malden, MA 02148, USA

ISBN-13: 978-0-7456-4752-4 (hardback)
ISBN-13: 978-0-7456-4753-1 (paperback)

A catalogue record for this book is available from the British Library.

Typeset in 11 on 13 pt Sabon
by Toppan Best-set Premedia Limited
Printed and bound in Great Britain by MPG Books Group Ltd, Bodmin, Cornwall

The publisher has used its best endeavours to ensure that the URLs for external websites referred to in this book are correct and active at the time of going to press. However, the publisher has no responsibility for the websites and can make no guarantee that a site will remain live or that the content is or will remain appropriate.

Every effort has been made to trace all copyright holders, but if any have been inadvertently overlooked the publisher will be pleased to include any necessary credits in any subsequent reprint or edition.

For further information on Polity, visit our website: www.politybooks.com

Contents

Acknowledgements

Sanjay Subrahmanyam first drew my attention to the Turkish chronicle which was the starting point for this book, and he has guided me through an East with which I was largely unfamiliar. Gilles Veinstein read a still very imperfect manuscript, pointing out gaps and errors, and he has been kind enough to share with me his own view of the Ottoman world.

The students, colleagues and friends who attend my seminar at the Ecole des hautes études des sciences sociales have discussed most of the pages which follow.

By her patient work as editor, combining professional skills and a deep understanding of the text, Agnès Fontaine helped to turn this manuscript into a book. Monique Labrune was kind enough to accept it into the series of which she is the general editor.

I thank them all.

Introduction

When in some regions it is daytime, in others it is night, and when in one region day breaks, in others night falls, so that when it is midday in Mexico, on the other side of the world, for those who live right under our feet, for them it is midnight, and when here the sun is rising, with them it is setting.

Henrico Martinez, *Repertorio de los tiempos*, p. 103

What Time is it There? is a history of worlds that encounter each other without ever meeting. It is the title of a film of Tsai Ming-liang which appeared in 2001. Since the end of the last century, Asian film-makers have never tired of exploring the transformations of the globe and of the imaginary. Koreans, Taiwanese, Chinese, Japanese, Indians or Thai, their films have accompanied or anticipated the effects of globalization[1] in this vast region of the world. *What Time is it There?* is one of those films that linger in the memory long after they have been seen. The plot is simple, almost too thin to be retold. In Taipei, a young Chinese woman stops at the stall of a vendor of watches and persuades him to sell her the one he has on his own wrist. She wants to have a watch that tells both Paris time and Taipei time. The street vendor learns that she is flying to France next day. Fascinated and attracted by his customer, the young man tries everything he can to get close to her and to abolish the distance and time that separates Taipei from Paris. He sets all the clocks in the Taiwanese capital to French time and he seeks out images of the City of Light. A video of Truffaut's *Quatre Cents Coups* (1959) opens a window onto the other world. And, while in Taipei the watch vendor dreams of being 'over there', the young woman wanders through the Paris of cafés, the metro and cemeteries, passing, without realizing it, Jean-Pierre Léaud, the unforgettable hero of Truffaut's film.

What Time is it There? plays on the irrepressible desire to conquer the barriers of space and time by abolishing the time difference and by inventing substitutes for a coveted elsewhere. The sequences follow one another without linking shots, emphasizing the fracture of a world torn between Taipei and Paris. Abortive meetings, coincidences without any follow-up and episodes with a bitter-sweet taste try fruitlessly to end the solitude of the young people by sketching an imaginary geography of what could link them one to the other.

Why do I begin with this film, which carries to perfection the art of ellipsis round a story too intimate or too banal to appear in any archive? *What Time is it There?* started me asking the questions which run through this book. It lays bare the unexpected emergence of other worlds, the sudden preoccupation with the Elsewhere, the rapid shrinking of distances and the confrontation of worlds; but also, and just as importantly, it reveals the irreducibility of temporalities and the watertightness of pasts and memories. For longer than is generally believed, this question – 'What time is it there?' – has opened up unexpected perspectives for instruction and enrichment, as well as causing pain to many individuals and civilizations. It is no accident that, in the films of Tsai Ming-liang, the juxtaposition and conjunction of worlds goes together with feelings of being torn and of heightened solitude. But incommunicability is not only an individual problem, it is a social issue, too.

Globalization is a paradoxical experience. It draws us into consumption habits, leisure activities and imaginaries that inextricably attach us one to the other. Films, radio, television, mobile phones and the Internet immerse us in a constant flow of news, images and fashions arriving from every part of the planet, so that now, if we are deprived of our daily ration of world news, we quickly feel a sense of loss; it is as if we can no longer ignore what is happening elsewhere, in other countries and among other peoples. Yet this constant feeling of immediacy and ubiquity is often no more than an illusion.

The increasing openness of our relationship to the world constantly comes up against old ways of feeling and of perceiving things. At the global level, day after day, new spaces of contention emerge which check the growth of a 'world consciousness' by recycling various fantasies and make-believes. The shadow of terrorism, the unthinking fear of Islam, the spectre of the American empire and all kinds of fundamentalist obsessions and apocalyptic panics, ecological or epidemiological – these are only some of the poisons which contaminate or block our approach to the world. They are all the more effective in that, though the Elsewhere may today be endlessly mediatized, it is still no better known nor any more familiar. New films remind us of this every week. For every *Babel* (Alejandro González Iñárritu, 2006), magisterially exploring the links between the different parts of the world, how many *Apocalypto* (Mel Gibson, 2007) or *300*s (Frank Miller, 2006) inundate us with nightmarish visions of the Other and Elsewhere.

'What time is it there?' I want in this book to explore this question more deeply, and show that it cannot be reduced to the cumulative and recent effects of communication technologies. On the contrary, it has precedents remote in time, on which a historical analysis can throw light. It is a consequence of the gradual dismantling of closed worlds, both physical and mental, long rooted in land, nation, race, religion or family; a dismantling which was hugely accelerated at the beginning of modern times, as revealed by the two testimonies I propose now to examine in depth, and which will require us to navigate between America and Islamic lands, long before the images of 11 September 2001 had entered our heads.

Belém do Pará, August 2005 – Paris, August 2007

– 1 –

Istanbul/Mexico City: The Eye of the Sages

> In the eye of wisdom, the seven regions of the world are like golden treasures. But if you look carefully, it is a serpent with seven heads.
>
> *Tarih-i Hind-i garbi*, p. 74

What time is it there? The Muslim East did not wait until the twenty-first century to become interested in America. Around 1580, on the shores of the Bosphorus, thoughtful people felt anxious about the New World, and they were by no means the first:

> It . . . became famous and known among men that now a new world is visible that is similar in width and circumference to regions of the inhabited quarter of the globe, and that, if not superior to the cultivated region in the number of inhabitants, is equal to it at least. Until this moment, no one in [= from] this region has visited that area nor has anyone given any information on its description. Hence, according to the saying 'relish things new', the favorably disposed soul flowed like a stream to those waters. The ship of thought dropped anchor in that sea.[1]

Istanbul Looks at Mexico City

In Istanbul, around 1580, when these words were written, Murâd III had been in power for six years. The Ottoman Empire was still at the height of its glory, even if the comet of 1577 and the assassination, two years later, of the Grand Vizier Sokollu Mehmed Pasha presaged more troubled times ahead. Since 1576 the Ottomans had been fighting against Persia, their enemy in the East. Their resounding victories on this front culminated in the annexation of Georgia and Azerbaijan. An Ottoman fleet would even patrol the Caspian Sea.[2] To the West, the Moroccans had defeated the Portuguese army of King Sebastian at the battle of Kasr al-Kabîr (1578). The victory over Lisbon, which gave the Porte cause to rejoice, would soon topple the world order, because it enabled King Philip II, two years later, to unite under the same sceptre the Spanish and Portuguese empires.

It was in these troubled times that an anonymous writer produced a long chronicle of the New World, to which various titles were given: 'Fresh News', 'A Book of the New Clime',[3] 'The First Appearance of the New World' and 'Announcement of the Event of the New World'.[4] I will follow its editor, Thomas Goodrich, in calling it *Tarih-i Hind-i garbi* (*A History of the India of the West*).[5] Its author lived in Istanbul, the old Constantinople, that 'so very delightful and convenient city, surely worthy, in its excellence and natural beauty, of being at the head of the empire of the whole world'.[6] We know almost nothing about him. Was he a protégé of Sokollu Mehmed Pasha and one of the astronomers associated with the construction of the great observatory of Murâd III? He may well have prudently preferred to remain in obscurity so as to avoid attracting the attention of the religious authorities who ordered the building to be demolished in 1580.

Everything suggests that this faceless chronicler moved in the entourage of the Grand Vizier and that he shared his expansionist views. Sokollu had been the initiator of an ambitious foreign policy, directed, in particular, at the Indian Ocean, with the aim of establishing a discreet but solid Ottoman presence in that part of Asia.[7] The name of the sultan was revered there, and his claim to universal monarchy increasingly recognized, even by the Great Mughal himself.[8] The author of the *Tarih-i Hind-i garbi* certainly belonged to a scholarly and well-read milieu, familiar with Arabic and Persian, but with access also to books and pieces of information or news written in Italian, Spanish and Portuguese.[9] It seems likely that this milieu was in contact with captured sailors or renegades from America, by way of the Iberian Peninsula and western Mediterranean and, even more, with escaped Marranos who had landed in Spain or Salonika. After their expulsion from Spain, decreed after the capture of Granada (1492), 'many Jews fled to Constantinople where they were given a warm welcome by the Great Sultan Bajazet (Bâyezîd II), and there was general amazement that the kings of Spain had expelled from their lands people so useful on the material plane'.[10] At least, this is what was being said and printed in Mexico City in the early years of the seventeenth century, some time before another expulsion, that of the Moriscos of Spain. Istanbul was also home to numerous Italians, Genoese, Venetians and Florentines, European merchants, ambassadors and artists. They were so strong a presence that our anonymous author must have been spoiled for choice of interlocutors.[11] Unless he himself was a renegade of Iberian or Italian origin?

But the Ottoman Empire was not Spain, and even less Christian Europe, where books about every part of the world were printed.[12] The *Tarih-i Hind-i garbi* was not published until 1730. It was the fourth work in Arabic characters to have this honour, since it was only in the eighteenth century that Istanbul adopted the invention of Gutenberg. In any case, the choice made by the printer Ibrahim Müteferrika, 150 years later, shows that this compendium of information about America retained its topicality. In fact many manuscript versions had been circulating since 1580, including at least four copies made from the original before the end of the sixteenth century.

The Turkish text stays so close to the narrative of the great Spanish chronicles of America that the Istanbul reader only had to put himself in the place of the conquistadors to discover the New World, the 'New India' as the Anonymous Chronicler called it. The voyages of Christopher Columbus, the conquest of the Caribbean, the invasion of Mexico and then that of Peru are described with a wealth of detail that would surprise anyone who still believed that the Ottoman Empire had turned its back on Spain and the Atlantic.[13] Mexico City, conquered by Hernán Cortés, appears as an amazing place, as worthy of intriguing the scholars of Istanbul as of fascinating the Castilian invaders sixty years before. After the Europeans who had devoured the Spanish accounts, the readers of the Anonymous Chronicler were invited to discover the palaces of Moctezuma. They could imagine the halls, the chambers and the baths that were counted in hundreds, they could visit the harem with a thousand wives, they could stroll through the gardens thickly sown with scented flowers and scattered with aviaries and pools and they could observe the cages that housed wild animals, 'tigers and lions and leopards [and] dragon-like snakes'; they could even enter the armoury jam-packed with bows, arrows and swords. The Turkish reader learned that the city of Mexico occupied an exceptional site:

It is all within a great lake whose circumference is about ninety *mils*. One-half of the aforementioned lake is salty . . . so that within it the creatures of the sea cannot live. One half is fresh, so that innumerable fish are within it . . . the city is in two districts. One of them is in the salty half. Moctezuma resides in that district. They call it Tlatelolco. One district is in the fresh-water half. They call it Mexico. Between the two districts are great bridges and numerous buildings. In the environs of the aforementioned lake there are fifty towns, some of which have ten thousand and some fifteen thousand homes.

As they worked their way through the chapters, among so much that was exotic, Turkish readers discovered the virtues of the *nopal* and the taste of the *nochtli*, which the Europeans called the Barbary fig: 'One kind is yellow . . . it is similar to the taste of a pear. One kind is white; it is like the grape in taste. One kind is pure vermilion: it ripens before all the others but it is not utterly delicious; it stains clothes and the skin fast.'[14]

Attention was not focused only on the city of Mexico. Drawn into the Southern hemisphere, the Istanbul readers discovered the empire of the Incas. They could glimpse Potosi, the mining city of the Andes, whose fabulous silver deposits could hardly fail to be of interest to the subjects of the Ottoman Empire, then flooded with American metal. Of equal interest was the sea route opened across the Pacific:

> In a book of the history books of the cursed Franks it is written that someone who ruled in the New World in the city of Mexico left Mexico in 1564 and passed around the earth and reached the land of China and the Spice Islands, which are around Hindistan and seized many of them. One of them is the island named Lukan (Luçon).[15]

The information may be incorrect, but this is clearly a reference to the expedition of López de Legazpi, which inaugurated the first regular connection between the Philippines (Luçon) and the coasts of Mexico.

So not only was the Atlantic Ocean – *Okyanus* 'in the language of Yunan' (the Greeks), Bahr-i Ahzer, 'the Green Sea', for the Turks – not that boundless and bottomless expanse spoken of by 'the Ancients of the Ulema', that is, the doctors of Muslim law, but a new continent existed; and this new continent contained rich kingdoms conquered and colonized by the Christians, *Yeni Ispanya*

(New Spain) in the North and *Peru* in the South. Miniatures adorn the various surviving copies of the *Tarih-i
Hind-i garbi*. They show how strange the New World
could seem to the inhabitants of the Old, including the
Turks. Counterpart of the emerging exoticism of European
artists, that of the Ottomans fastened on the most singular
animals and plants of American nature, such as manatees,
tapirs, turkeys, bison, jaguars, avocados and papayas. The
city of Potosi even inspired a series of miniatures which
reveal how artists in Istanbul imagined the agglomerations
of the 'New India'.[16] In most of the Ottoman manuscripts
the mining city has the appearance of a strongly fortified
town, very different from the little market town huddled
at the foot of the mountain that is shown in the Italian
edition of the chronicle of Cieza de Léon (Rome, 1555).
The miniaturists of Istanbul took as many liberties with
American reality as did the European artists of the
Renaissance.

Istanbul Seen from Mexico City

What time is it there? In Mexico, at the beginning of the
seventeenth century, people began to be interested in the
Ottoman Empire. A printer, Heinrich Martin, set out to
satisfy the curiosity of readers in New Spain by publishing
a *Repertorio de los tiempos* (*Repertory of the Times,*
1606), two chapters of which were devoted to the history
of the Ottoman world. The first, which is fiercely committed, 'treats of the way in which one deduces from predictions, prognoses, conjectures and natural reasons the fall
and the destruction of the monarchy and the empire of the
Turks'; the second, which is relatively dispassionate,
explains 'the origins of the Turkish Empire, and the way
in which it grew and in which it achieved the power it
wields today'.[17] There are no illustrations in this history
of the Turks to guide the imagination of the reader, who
had to fall back on the memories left by local festivities in

which Moors and Turks had featured. A few years before the appearance of the *Repertorio*, to celebrate the arrival of the new viceroy, the Count of Monterrey, some notables of the town had disguised themselves as Turkish knights, 'sporting blue cloaks' in the Moorish fashion; they then attacked a mock castle erected for the occasion in the small town of Guadalupe, on the edge of the lagoon, at the entry to the capital.[18] Knights of Malta, played by other Spaniards, had defended the site with the success one would expect. The authenticity of the costumes may have left something to be desired by our standards, but not, we may be sure, the impact of these images on those who watched or participated in these mock battles.

Much more is known about the career of Heinrich Martin than about that of his homologue in Istanbul. Historians have made him a Spaniard from Andalusia, a Portuguese from Ayamonte, a Fleming, a Frenchman and even a Creole, who would therefore have been born in Mexico. In fact he was a German, born in Hamburg around 1560.[19] This great northern port had embraced the Reformation some thirty years earlier and it is likely that the family of Heinrich Martin was Lutheran. In any case, at the age of eight, the young boy was sent to Seville, to a family of German printers who also bore the name of Martin. Heinrich spent his boyhood and adolescence on the banks of the Guadalquivir, being initiated into the trade of printer. When he was about nineteen he returned to Hamburg, where he lived for a year and a half: 'Out of curiosity, he visited the churches, which all belonged to Lutheran heretics . . . on Sundays and at Easter, because they were the only feasts that they observed then.'[20] A strange curiosity, because he frequented the temples of Satan at the time of services; forty years later, however, it seems to have aroused little curiosity on the part of the Inquisition of Mexico, when it came by this information.

At the age of twenty, Heinrich began to travel in Europe. He studied mathematics in Paris before moving to

Courland (Latvia) and probably also Poland. Since the 1570s this kingdom had been a haven of peace to which heretics of every sort flocked, Calvinists, Lutherans, 'Polish Brethren', anti-Trinitarians with Anabaptist leanings and even 'non-adorers', so called because they refused to adore Jesus Christ.[21] It is hard to imagine that the young Heinrich did not also indulge his curiosity in the churches of Poland. The king, Stefan Batori, was at this period supporting the Jesuits and making his kingdom a laboratory for the Counter-Reformation. He even aspired to make it a bridgehead against the Turks. A former Voivode of Transylvania, Batori hoped that his victorious campaigns against the Muscovites (1579–81) would help him to launch a vast offensive against Istanbul. He died in 1586 before he had been able to embark on his project. It was probably in this context that Heinrich Martin became aware of the power of and the threat posed by the Ottoman Empire.[22]

What did Martin do next on the borders of Europe, having renewed contact in Hamburg with the Lutheranism which had surrounded him in his childhood? Act as an agent for the merchants of the great Hanse port? Pursue his studies of mathematics and astronomy in the universities of Krakow or Königsberg? Work in a printing house in Krakow or Vilnius? Get involved in the work preparatory to the compilation of the maps commissioned by King Stefan, in particular those of Lithuania and Livonia?[23] There is no shortage of possibilities, but nothing is known. The motive for his interest in Courland is equally mysterious. One can only imagine a business trip to Riga to explain his presence in this out-of-the-way country.[24] Did he go there with the intention of opening a printing house, as he was to do later in Mexico? The book trade between Germany and the Baltic countries was prospering; it was a dangerous but tempting activity at this period of religious turbulence.[25] A Catholic Heinrich Martin might have assisted the publishing activities of the Jesuit Possevino; a Lutheran Heinrich Martin might equally well have collaborated with Protestant printers.[26]

Almost all that we know of his time in Courland are the quasi-ethnographical observations he recorded later, in Mexico, in his *Repertorio de los tiempos*: 'This province is populated by people of the same appearance, condition and character as the Indians of this New Spain, except that they are a little more corpulent like the Chichimecas and they speak a different language than that used by the populations of the neighbouring countries. It is certainly true that it is surprising to see these brown and submissive people when the populations of the neighbouring provinces are white, red-haired and bellicose, which is why I think that those people there and these here are the same people, and what makes me readier to believe this is that at this latitude there is little distance between the regions here [in Mexico] and those of Asia and Europe.'[27]

After his travels in Europe, Martin returned to Spain, where he spent several years in transit between Madrid, Toledo and Seville. In the capital, he acquired typographical equipment, but there is no evidence that he opened a printing house in Castile. In 1589, having reached the age of thirty, he embarked for the New World with the fleet of Luis de Velasco, the new viceroy of Mexico. The regular departures of viceroys for the Indies attracted all sorts of people to make the crossing, since all that was needed, to join the voyage, was the protection of the happy appointee.[28] The father of the new viceroy had ruled over New Spain and the Velasco family had close links with Mexican society. Luis' support was therefore a doubly valuable 'open sesame'. Nevertheless, we know neither how Martin got involved in this milieu nor what led him to leave for America or, even more, decide to stay there.

Heinrich Martin had many strings to his bow. Trained as a printer at an early age in Seville and in other towns in Spain, he seems to have embarked for America equipped with all that was needed to open a printing house in the New World. However, it was only in 1599, ten years after his arrival, that he set up in business.[29] He also held a title of royal cosmographer, no doubt procured thanks to the mathematical training acquired in Paris or in other European cities.[30] In Mexico City, after 1598, Martin became a zealous collaborator of the Holy Office.[31] This earned him custody of the goods of a Dutch printer arrested by the Inquisition on suspicion of Lutheranism, and he was subsequently able to take over the suspect's presses. Accustomed to putting his linguistic skills at the service of the inquisitors, our German landed the grandiloquent title of 'interpreter of the Holy Office for the Flemish and German language', with all the 'favours, franchises, exceptions and liberties' attached to this office.[32] They included the right to bear arms day and night, evidence that his duties in connection with the Inquisition were not entirely risk free.

As a printer Heinrich Martin had many other ways of demonstrating his support for the Counter-Reformation. He published religious works and funeral orations, he collaborated closely with the University of Mexico, the Dominicans and the Jesuits and he developed friendships with intellectuals of the stature of Antonio Rubio and Antonio Arias.[33] The educated circles of the Mexican capital adopted a man who would print selected passages for the use of the masters and pupils of the Society of Jesus, such as the *Poeticarum Institutionum* of 1605, an invaluable introduction to the mysteries of Latin poetry. This successful integration did not prevent him from casting a merciless gaze at the society which welcomed him: 'Here, as we all know, the lure of gain prevails to such an extent that curiosity is in a sense excluded, because curiosity and cupidity are two things opposed at every point.'[34]

Heinrich Martin was himself the author of a scientific work. When, in 1606, he published his *Repertorio de los tiempos* on his own presses, the highest authorities in New Spain gave him their support: the viceroy, the Marquis of Montesclaros, appreciated the 'agreeable [style] and Christian modesty' of such an 'interesting and useful' work, which was also 'beneficial to the whole republic, in particular farmers'. The doctor of theology, Hernando Franco Risueño, and the archbishop of Mexico, García de Mendoza, were delighted to find in it 'things that are so interesting and that it is essential to know in this new world'. Two years earlier, Martin had published a *Discourse on the Great Conjunction of the Planets Jupiter and Saturn*, a more modest text, of which he was also the author. Two big treatises, one on agriculture in New Spain and the other on physiognomy, either never progressed beyond the planning stage or remained in manuscript.[35]

After publishing his *Repertorio*, Martin was entrusted with a mammoth task, the direction of the works to drain the Valley of Mexico, to which he devoted more than twenty years of his life. He was one of the Europeans of the late Renaissance most directly involved in a major civil engineering project; this won him the admiration of the playwright Ruiz de Alarcón, who chose to sing his praises before the Spanish public in one of his finest works: 'It is only right that we should exalt/so remarkable a marvel/as foremost in the world.'[36] This crushing burden changed Heinrich Martin's life and its difficulties probably hastened his end. He died loathed by some among his contemporaries, accused of having allowed Mexico City to be flooded rather than see the massive works for which he had been responsible swept away by the water.

Mirror Effects

In the age of the Internet and the mobile phone, caught up in the backwash of a globalization whose effects are still largely unknown, it may come as a surprise that people in Mexico, four centuries ago, were interested in Turkey, and not only in Spain and Peru. In fact, while Istanbul, with nearly 400,000 inhabitants, was then the biggest city in Europe,[37] Mexico City dominated the New World. It had more than 100,000 inhabitants, a court, a university, colleges and massive convents, a well-educated clergy and prosperous merchants. It was one of the jewels in the crown of the Catholic monarchy, which had united, since 1580, the Spanish and Portuguese Empires. It may seem even more surprising that an inhabitant of Istanbul should have tried to find out everything he could about the discovery, conquest and colonization of the New World by the 'Franks'; and that he should have turned, to this end, to the best historians of the day, the Italian Peter Martyr d'Anghiera and the Castilians Gonzalo Fernández de Oviedo, Francisco López de Gómara and Agustín de Zarate, names which had revealed the New World to the Europe of the Renaissance.[38] These same sources had been used by the Dutch to learn about America and the Great Discoveries. In his preface, our Istanbul chronicler does not conceal the urgency of his task: 'The ancient writing and earlier books do not comment on [the New World] and do not undertake their explanation, and the greatest experts among the authorities of history do not even touch . . . these things. Therefore . . . I collected some responsible truthful books and recent maps . . . and after translating and commenting on them in general, a summary was set forth and written down.'[39]

Istanbul–Mexico City: it is not without interest that these were both young cities that had been grafted onto prestigious capitals: Spanish Mexico City developed in the Aztec capital from 1521 and Ottoman Istanbul had replaced Byzantium in 1453. Nevertheless, seen from western Europe, these two metropolises ordinarily appear as 'exotic peripheries', one a product of Spanish colonization implanted on a fallen empire, the other an outpost of a fascinating and intrusive East. This is to forget that these new actors on the Renaissance scene occupied privileged positions at points where worlds met: Amerindians, Iberians and Asiatics in the case of Mexico City, Europeans, Africans and Asiatics in that of Istanbul. If Mexico City incarnated the American impact of Iberian globalization, Istanbul synthesized the equally planetary dynamism of the societies of Islam. In both West and East these cities acted as intermediaries and couriers between societies as diverse as they were remote from each other, mapping out a geography which historians have done little to make familiar to us, so concerned have they been to separate histories, empires and cultural zones.

The Shock of the Sources

Our ways of doing history still often confine us within such narrow and fragmented, not to say distorted, visions of the past that, even today, to compare Turkish and Mexican sources seems to border on some sort of pyrotechnic display or conjuring trick. Yet these sources are known, translated and published, hence easily accessible.[40] Manuscripts of the Turkish chronicle are found in several western libraries, including the Bibliothèque nationale de France; the *Repertorio de los tiempos* was published in Mexico three times in the second half of the twentieth century.[41]

However the historian's task cannot consist simply of exhuming Mexican or Turkish histories in order to exhibit them as historiographical aberrations or exotic curiosities. It needs to be explained why certain Turks were able to know more about America than many Orientalists today, and why readers in Mexico City asked questions about the Ottomans that have never crossed the minds of the Americanists. The two worlds were not in direct contact. It is unlikely that any Turks visited New Spain in the sixteenth century, or that any inhabitants of Mexico had been in contact with Istanbul. There is no link, therefore, between the two texts. Turkish or Mexican, each is an expression of the world which produced it, mixed with images of the world it describes. It is precisely this mixing and this parallelism that made me decide to compare them, though without seeking to do this too literally, in a way that would quickly risk verging on the absurd. What would be the point of asking if the Turks knew more about the Mexicans than the Mexicans about the Turks? Or if the author in Mexico City was more 'open', and hence more 'modern', than the author in Istanbul, or if chocolate tastes better than coffee?[42] Are the sources for the Mexican *Repertorio* more reliable than those for the Turkish chronicle? It would have been fascinating to imagine a direct Mexico City–Istanbul dialogue above the heads of western Europe, but such an exchange seems never to have taken place. On the other hand, the Italian presses of the Renaissance and the language of Ariosto played the role of intercontinental 'resonance chambers'. Without the Italy of humanists, scholars and printers, there would have been no *Tarih-i Hind-i garbi*, nor even a *Repertorio*.[43]

In fact, placed side by side, the two works irresistibly evoke the sequence shots of the film of Tsai Ming-liang. Mexico City/Istanbul . . . Paris/Taipei . . . The narratives are independent, but juxtaposing them immediately raises all sorts of questions. One wants to check each text against the other so as to bring out more clearly the respective peculiarities of the two visions, as if the biases of the Turkish chronicle could help us to ask better questions of the Mexican work, and as if it, in its turn, would help to guide us through the complexities of the Ottoman text. It is for me to 'show' them together in the manner of the Taiwanese film director, in order to imagine, over and above the differences which divided these universes, or rather by drawing on the tensions between them, what 'thinking the world' could mean at the end of the Renaissance; in the hope, to paraphrase the formula of S. M. Eisenstein, that 'the juxtaposition of those very elements . . . shall evoke in the perception and feelings of [the reader] the most complete image of the theme itself'.[44] So, if we juxtapose these two texts, what does it tell us about scholars, cities and societies which a priori everything separated – seas, religions, memories, histories? And what does it also tell us about the links which may already have united Islamic lands and America?

– 2 –

'What Time is it There?'

It is no longer in doubt that beneath the Equator and beneath the poles there live the same multitude of people as in all the other parts of the world.

> Giovanni Battista Ramusio, *Discorso sopra il terzo volume delle navigationi et viaggi*
> (Venice, 1556)

What characterizes *by nature* almost all human beings without exception is this common and universal inclination and capacity to ignore, without any sense of being at fault, the majority of human beings living outside their own ethnic catchment area.

> Peter Sloterdijk, *Sphären II*

Today, the omnipresence of the media instils in us all the illusion that we are as much witnesses as contemporaries of world events. What was it like at the end of the sixteenth century? When readers in Mexico City, Spanish, mestizo and Indian elites, worried about the fate of the Ottoman Empire, and when men of letters in Istanbul feared for the future of the 'New India' fallen beneath the yoke of the 'Franks', that is, the Spanish, it is clear that all of them were already beginning to belong to the same planet and share the same horizons. It hardly matters that their viewpoints differed or that their analyses led them to opposite conclusions. The proliferation of copies of the *Tarih-i Hind-i garbi,* and the printing in Mexico of the *Repertorio de los tiempos* at a time when the publication of a book in America remained a rare, expensive and carefully considered act, were significant initiatives. They expressed a curiosity that was genuine and often of long standing, quite the opposite of a sudden fad or burst of exoticism.

A World 'Everywhere Inhabited'

'We are clearly given to understand that this earthly globe is everywhere marvellously inhabited, no part is empty or without inhabitants, either on account of the heat or the cold.'[1] This is how, in the mid sixteenth century, a Venetian publisher of travel stories commented on the prodigious shrinking of horizons brought about by the great voyages of discovery. In whatever continent they made their home, people lived under the same heaven, as a Jesuit of Peru observed to some Spaniards who had settled in the Andes but sighed for the skies of Spain.[2]

The possibilities opened up by navigation transformed communications between peoples. The Portuguese, the Spanish and the Italians were not the only ones to realize this. All those who, at one time or another, found themselves face-to-face with Europeans frequently had bitter experience of it. The worlds of Islam paid close attention, therefore, and with good reason, to the arrival of the Portuguese in the Indian Ocean and south-east Asia. Though they did not choose the way of conquest, the Ottomans were not slow to react. By the beginning of the sixteenth century their fleet was making its presence known in the waters of the Indian Ocean. In the 1560s Suleiman the Magnificent negotiated an alliance with the Sultan of Aceh, a rising kingdom in the north of the island of Sumatra, so as to help him to fend off the claims of Lisbon in this part of the world.[3] One after another the populations and powers of Asia crossed swords with the Portuguese who circulated off their coasts. No country, be it China, Japan, Siam or Cambodia, could ignore this intrusive proximity.

In addition to which a new horizon emerged in the East as the sixteenth century progressed, beyond that immense ocean in which Spanish vessels returning from the New World suddenly appeared. Since Magellan's circumnavigation of the globe (1521), the Pacific Ocean (*Derya-i Sur, Bahr-i Muhit-i Sur* for the Turks)[4] had been poised to become a route which united America and Asia. But Asia had made its appearance on the horizons of the New World even before the New World loomed on those of Asia. America, recognized as a separate continent, had ceased to be an immense raft of lands isolated from the rest of the world. It had been colonized by the Europe of the Iberians, linked up with the Africa of slaves and connected, via Manila and the Philippines, to Japan and to China. Before the Great Discoveries, 'the earth could not be fully known, or the peoples communicate with one another'.[5] Those times were gone for ever.

Wherever you were, maritime communications acquired crucial importance. The Anonymous Chronicler of Istanbul was as interested in the circumnavigation of Magellan as in the cutting of a canal between the Red Sea and the Mediterranean, a pet project in the political circles in which he moved.[6] His approach was never simply anecdotal. He described Magellan's voyage with a grasp of both its geographical and its political implications: 'From the countries of Portugal [there was] a corsair whom they called Ferdinand Magellan. He had learned from some philosophers that it was possible to reach the Moluccas, that is, the spice islands, by way of the Western Ocean.' If this new route eluded the Ottomans, they retained the possibility of joining the waters of the Mediterranean to those of the Indian Ocean. Why open a canal towards the 'sea of Kulzum', the Red Sea, if not to take the Persians from the rear, protect Mecca and cleanse the Indian Ocean?

> Thenceforth from the well-protected Constantinople, the place of prosperity and the place of the throne of the sultanate, ships and crew would be organized and sent to the sea of Kulzum and would have the power to protect the shores of the Holy Places. And in a short time . . . they would seize most of the seaports of Sind and Hind and would drive away and expel from that region the evil unbelievers.[7]

If this programme was included in a text devoted to the subject of America, it is because the author was aware that the New World had become a bridge to Asia, hence a threat to Islam in this part of the world.

Mexico City did not lag behind. Though not remotely comparable to Constantinople, except perhaps in its past grandeur, it was certainly not some small town of pioneers buried away in the middle of an indigenous America. Home to a Spanish court, a university and an archbishopric, the largest city in the New World aspired to be the centre of the universe. Subject by all sorts of ties to the Iberian metropolis, the capital of New Spain was in regular contact with the Caribbean, with Equatorial Africa and with Central America and Peru. But it was still drawn towards the West, too, towards the Asia of missionaries, merchants and conquerors.[8] Did the young Spaniards who lived in Mexico not dream of seizing the riches of the Orient? And are there not faint echoes of the Crusades in the lines of the poet Bernardo de Balbuena's *Grandeza mexicana*?

> O! valorous and crowned Spain
> . . . See, on the eastern squadrons
> Of India and of Malabar, of Japan and China,
> Your victorious banners wave;
> And your mounts drink

The foamy and crystalline water
Of the Indus and the Ganges,
And Mount Imabo bows before your grandeur.[9]

While some, on the iridescent shores of the Bosphorus, imagined the city of Moctezuma, others, in the shade of the palaces and cloisters of Mexico City, speculated about the ruin and the grandeur of Constantinople. And all of them dreamed of the East. In both cities, the imagination of the poets and their readers could still be stirred by fabulous countries and intoxicated by unknown shores and bottomless oceans. The Spanish in Mexico were able to feed their dreams from the *Lusiads* of Camões, a magnificent epic poem, echoes of which permeate the verse of Balbuena, as if Mexico, too, saw itself in the mirror of Goa.

But enough of dreams. In both Mexico City and Istanbul people had access to an ever-larger body of increasingly reliable information with which to be united in an uninhibited imperialism with no limits to its horizons. From one place or another they procured sources that were solid, or claimed to be, they collected images, they assembled measurements and figures, they accumulated geographical facts and they investigated creatures, fauna and flora. Christian or Muslim, how could they resist the lure of distant riches? 'The exquisite things of Sind and Hind and the rarities of Ethiopia and the Sudan . . . the pearls of Bahrain and the pearls of Aden' enthralled our anonymous author of Istanbul, just as the 'diamonds of India . . . the amber of Malabar, the pearls of the Hydaspes and the drugs of Egypt' excited the poet of Mexico and his readers.[10] Such covetousness explains why the new relationships between worlds did nothing to abolish the antagonisms and hatreds of the past. As the ambitions of governments acquired a planetary resonance and basis, these all-consuming drives became one of the motors, real or virtual, of the imperialisms then rampant in the world.

Interest in the World

A race for gold and silver, a race for spices and precious stones . . . In the sixteenth century Europeans of a new type cared about the world for reasons which may seem to us basely materialist, not to say shaped by expansionist obsessions or by even more disturbing impulses when the siren-song of messianism and millenarianism was heard. I will return to this.[11] But are these motives enough to explain the growing interest in events in remote parts? These preoccupations have also been seen as revealing the beginnings of ethnological observation or as expressing an innate gift for grasping cultural diversity. Putting aside the considerable dose of Eurocentrism implied by this last explanation, is it satisfying?[12] Whether well-founded or not, all these explanations seem to me reductive. If we are too preoccupied with absolving or condemning the past, we risk losing sight of what constituted its singularity, and perhaps also its value for us.

Contemporaries, who were no less well placed than we to understand what was happening to them, often found striking phrases for commenting on the opening up to the world in which they participated. In 1552 the chronicler of the Indies, Francisco López de Gómara, wrote:

> The world is so large and so beautiful and it contains so many things different one from the other that it amazes whoever considers it and contemplates it. There are few men, if they no longer live like beasts, who do not one day begin to consider its marvels, because the desire to know is something natural to us all. But some feel this desire more strongly than others because they have added to natural inclination their skill and their effort; and they understand better the secrets and the causes of the things which nature produces.[13]

Deseo de saber, the desire to know: the phrase seems anachronistic but it is certainly there in the texts. This desire encouraged an openness to the world that was almost boundless. It went together with another desire, that 'to see the world' in the name of the greatest possible 'freedom'.[14] No country could escape this *deseo de saber*, even the Ultima Thule which had appeared in Seneca's *Medea* as the furthest frontier of the known world.

How far back does this desire go in Latin Christendom? At least to the thirteenth century, when the stories brought back from Mongol Asia began to awaken, or reawaken, this interest in Europeans.[15] A flurry of travel stories accompanied the first opening up of Latin Christendom to the world. This was still without thought of conquest, its aims being more missionary and commercial, so impotent did Christendom feel in the face of the Mongol giant. It was in this context that Marco Polo, and others with him, revealed to Europeans the complexities of the Asian world, from central Asia to Cathay and the fabulous Japan.

It was not only the Italians and the French who opened their eyes. Though they lived at the other end of the Mediterranean, and were still preoccupied with their struggle against the Moors, the Christians of the Iberian Peninsula were curious in their turn about what was happening in Asia. At the very beginning of the fifteenth century a Castilian ambassador to the Mongol Tamerlaine returned with a report remarkable for its freshness and wisdom.[16] By this period Iberians felt sufficiently equipped to explore and describe distant lands. This was not true only of the Portuguese who visited the coasts of Africa; long before any Castilians had set foot in Mexico, an Andalusian hidalgo, Pedro Tafur, had observed and indulged his curiosity in the Near East. The routes of Africa and the Indian Ocean were not only of interest to the sailors of Lisbon. It was possible to set out to conquer the West, following in the footsteps of Christopher Columbus, with one eye kept firmly fixed on the East of spices and the gold of Africa; by 1512, twenty years after the discovery of America, Portuguese expeditions to Asia led to the publication in Spain of a work devoted to 'the conquest of India, Persia and Arabia'.[17]

It remains the case that the sailors of Lisbon were the pioneers. The Portuguese advances into the unknown, the crossing of spaces reputed to be unfit for human life – the torrid zone, the Antipodes – and the explorations which punctuated the interminable descent of the shores of Africa had to overcome a host of fears, ignorance and prejudice: what monsters, what sub-human creatures, what devilish traps might suddenly loom up in these unknown worlds? The physical, technical and climatic obstacles were equally numerous. As soon as one confronted the realities of the terrain, interest in the distant world and seas turned into a high-risk enterprise. But this interest still continued to grow, with the unprecedented mobility acquired by Europeans during the sixteenth century, and with them all those who accompanied them, willingly or not: 'Men cross the Ocean Sea nowadays, from whatever point on one side to whatever point on the other that they wish, which they do with incredible speed and accuracy.'[18] Every discovery was seen as a further opportunity to strengthen links between peoples: 'With time', we read, in a work on nautical technique published in Mexico in 1587, 'thanks to the Strait of Magellan, the many known lands, islands and peoples and the infinite number of all those not yet known in the South Sea [the Pacific] could make contact with those of the North Sea [the Atlantic]'.[19] For the author of the massive compilation given the title *Navigations and Travels*, the Venetian Ramusio (1485–1557), it was astonishing

> that no one has reminded the princes and great men, those to whom God has given this responsibility, and who always surround themselves in their councils with men remarkable for their culture and intelligence, that one of the most admirable and amazing enterprises that they could undertake in their life would be to act so that all the people of our hemisphere *would come to know* all those of the opposite hemisphere, where they would pass for gods, as

was the case, for the Ancients, with Hercules and Alexander, who only crossed into India; and this unprecedented enterprise would far surpass all those of Julius Caesar and any other Roman emperor.[20]

One could only gain in prestige from discovering the world. Istanbul believed this, too. When the Anonymous Chronicler drew attention to Arabo-Andalusian precedents for the discovery of the New World, it was because he was trying by every means at his disposal to minimize the backwardness of the sailors of Islam; as if the Muslims of Spain had also, in their day, taken their share of the risks and thrown themselves into the race for discoveries, disregarding the Ancients who had claimed that the journey was impossible.[21]

The desire to know was universal. Portuguese, Italians, Spaniards and, to a lesser degree, English, Dutch and French interested themselves in the new spaces they were becoming used to visiting or colonizing, while at the same time keeping a close eye on the terrestrial and maritime power which threatened and fascinated Europeans most, the Ottoman Empire. The parallelism is striking. The increasing curiosity about the Turkish world was contemporary with the Portuguese penetration of Asia and the Spanish discovery of the New World. The interest varied, it is true, according to the European country. While Spain and Portugal wrote and published mostly on their own empires, in sixteenth-century France more works were printed on Turkey than on the New World, whereas Italy, in particular Venice, publicized all the discoveries and all the travellers indiscriminately.[22]

Taking the World in Hand

That this desire to know, extending to the whole world, was the accompaniment to a nascent imperialism, and that it was an expression of, or alibi for, the greed aroused by the riches promised by distant worlds, is clear. That it expressed a taste for risk coupled with an unstoppable mobility, and that it revealed a thirst for prestige and fame mixed with great openness, is now apparent to all. But these ventures also revealed a recurrent obsession among the Iberians with taking local populations in hand. 'The Barbarians are our neighbours and as such we have a duty to do good to them', explained Francisco de Vitoria in his *Relectiones* of Salamanca (1539).[23] As for the Indians of America, new converts to the faith, they ought to be raised like children, 'with milk and light, easily digestible dishes, suited to their limited capacity and to the short time they have been within the Christian religion'.[24] This is a paternalism, even a maternalism, which is far from having disappeared from the contemporary world, where it often finds expression in the interventionism of the great international institutions or the proliferation of NGOs.

The roots of this voluntarism were fundamentally religious. 'God', the same Vitoria emphasized, 'has ordained that everyone should care for their neighbour . . . they are our neighbours and we have a duty to labour for their benefit'.[25] The papacy, in the second half of the fifteenth century, had entrusted the Iberian sovereigns with the global mission of taking the peoples of the world in hand, wherever and whoever they were, so as to provide for their salvation; now, in the sixteenth century, for the first time in history, the sudden increase in connections between Europe and the other continents made this possible:

> Not without good reason or deep mystery the most rejected lineage and the most distant of men are specially called to the good of the Gospel . . . It is certain that St John in the Apocalypse . . . has made us see, in this blessed multitude who follow the Lamb, all the peoples, all the tribes and all the languages which exist under the sky.[26]

This concern for the other, which had repercussions that were often damaging to the 'beneficiaries', be they human beings, plants or ecosystems, manifested itself in many ways. It was apparent both in the great evangelizing projects orchestrated by the emissaries of Roman Catholicism and in the debate about the status and origins of the peoples of the continent of America. When the lawyers and politicians of the sixteenth century reflected on the freedom of the Indians and the legitimacy of the wars waged against them, the debate boiled down to the definition of acceptable ways of taking the newly subject peoples in hand. Already, almost a century earlier, the bull *Romanus Pontifex* (1454), promulgated to accompany the first Portuguese discoveries, had stipulated that the paternal responsibility for all the regions of the world lay with the Holy See.[27] It was because the papacy had been able to dictate with an almost inspired prescience the programme for Iberian expansion that it appears today as the 'notary' of the globalization that began in the fifteenth century.[28]

However, the concern of Christendom was not confined to the present and future fate of the creatures it encountered; it extended to ensuring that their past was integrated into the history of the world. For many centuries the question of the origins of the Indians of America – an abstract debate apparently far removed from any present contingencies – inspired the most diverse, and sometimes most foolish, hypotheses. It is as if educated Europeans were horrified that the history of a part of the world might resist them by presenting insoluble puzzles: Atlantis, the reappearance of the Ten Lost Tribes of Israel, a Carthaginian conquest of the New World – anything would serve as long as it dispelled the mystery.[29]

It is this intrusive interest in the Elsewhere, focusing on all the ways it could be appropriated, that lay behind the organization of the first European scientific projects, such as the mission entrusted to the physician Francisco Hernández, in the 1570s, to inventory the plants, animals and minerals of the West Indies; or the investigations that led to the compilation of the *Relaciones Geográficas* (*Geographical Reports*), which listed the natural and human

resources of the Hispano-American lands, inquired about
the way of life of the Indians, scoured the local histories
and amassed vast quantities of information which far
exceeded the needs of the Spanish administration or its
capacity to absorb it. Not content with specifying the
geographical coordinates of the places they described, the
researchers wanted to know everything about their inhabitants as well.[30]

This was surely the first time in European history that
the needs of science, economics or politics mobilized means
on such a scale outside the continent. What time is it in
Cuzco when it is nine o'clock in the evening in Sicily?
Midday, was the unhesitating reply of a Spanish astronomer, who got it wrong by a mere three hours. The measures of longitude still left much to be desired, but they
gave concrete expression to the desire to achieve a syn-
chronic view of the world. It was by observing lunar
eclipses in Europe, America and Asia (most notably
in 1577, and then in 1584) that Iberian scholars
reached some first results and, above all, learned how to
carry out coordinated operations in different parts of the
planet.[31]

Looking in Every Direction

Interest grew and shifted focus in line with European penetration and the progress of Iberian globalization. At a
very early stage it was no longer only the Europe of Lisbon,
Seville and Rome which was casting glances far afield, but
the Portuguese of Goa who were concerned about the
African and Asian peoples who lived along the shores of
the Indian Ocean, and even the masters of Spanish America
who were eyeing the islands of the Pacific, the Moluccas
and the coasts of China and Japan. And in its turn, in a
neat and rapid reversal of things, the New World worried
about the Old. Scarcely had Hernán Cortés completed the
conquest of Mexico than he was assuring the Emperor

Charles V of his support against the Turks. Rumour and news already circulated rapidly throughout the world:

> We have heard talk *here* of the assemblies of people organized by your Majesty to counter the Turk and resist him, because, it is said, he is full of power and pride. We all hope that God will assist such a Catholic enterprise, as he has done in everything that has happened since your Majesty came to the throne. The religious who live *in these countries* have not ceased and do not cease to pray and they say *here* that all the Christian kings and lordships are allied with your Majesty and matters are so well arranged that . . . if it please God, we will hear good and joyous news. I assure your Majesty that there is nothing I desire more in the world than to be of service in this expedition and be counted in the number of faithful vassals who are gathered there.[32]

The preparations for a crusade were discussed in Mexico City just as they had once been discussed in London, Bruges and Paris. And it was not only a matter of empty words or arm's length support. In 1541, eight years after the above letter was written and twenty years after the fall of Mexico City, Cortés did indeed accompany Charles V on the expedition to Algeria. Neither Mexican affairs nor the exploration of the Pacific nor the route to Asia could distract the aging conquistador from events in the Mediterranean.

If the pace of discovery slowed, impatience increased. This was the case with the island of San Lorenzo (Madagascar):

> It is bigger than the kingdom of Castile and Portugal . . . it is densely populated by reason of its temperate climate and the abundance of everything human beings have need of to live; it is one the most noble and most excellent of islands that have been discovered in our time. From this island people have so far wanted to explore only a few sea ports and all the rest remains unknown. It is the same for

a large part of Taprobane Island, for Java, la Grande and la Petite, and for an infinite number of others.[33]

This passionate interest in distant lands strikes us today as excessive and unrealistic. Simultaneously attention, obsession and tension, it ignored the obstacles presented by the oceans as well as by the most elementary requirements of realpolitik. Nothing seemed inaccessible to the Iberians, even China, the greatest empire on earth. Once Spain was firmly established in Manila, in the Philippines (1571), missionaries, bishops, judges and representatives of the Crown began to devise projects for conquering China and Japan. In quick succession, the bishop of Manila, the bishop of Malacca and the governor of the Philippines made passionate pleas for military intervention. In their minds, the archipelago began to resemble a military base, on the model of Naples or Flanders. And it was not only in Spanish Manila and Portuguese Malacca that people dreamed of an invasion.[34] In Mexico City, in the spring of 1587, there were fierce arguments about the appropriateness of declaring war on this land located at the end of the world.[35] All sorts of more or less specious rights and reasons were debated that would justify armed intervention: the urgency of converting China, the right of free circulation and free trade which the Iberians claimed everywhere in the world,[36] the pope's spiritual jurisdiction over the whole of humanity, the power that was his to change governments at will, and so on. For the bellicose party, the Chinese refusal to open up to foreigners, the fact of 'not admitting to this country any other nation, even one that wished to enter peacefully, but on the contrary to prohibit everyone from frequenting or trading with it' amounted to an unarguable *casus belli*. Firmly convinced of the opposite, the Jesuit José de Acosta struggled to make the warmongers see reason. Although he finally won his cause, the intensity of his pleading reveals the strength of the relentless energy which drove the Spanish towards the most improbable and least justifiable of objectives.

Conversar, contratar, convertir, conquistar: to frequent, to trade, to convert, to conquer, the slippage from one to the other was unstoppable. The idea that a country could remain impermeable to European penetration, even in principle entirely peaceful, was felt as intolerable. The further away the Iberians were from the European continent, the more they were seduced by global projects. It was true of the Spanish of Mexico and of the Portuguese of Goa, who pictured themselves conquering South Africa so as to seize its fabulous silver mines.[37] It was a paradoxical reaction, since it was those who were best-informed, established on the peripheries of the Catholic monarchy, who pressed for these unrealistic schemes, while in Madrid and Lisbon they preached caution.

The Sin of Indifference

Did one have the right not to know? In Istanbul, in the circles around the Anonymous Chronicler, no one could understand how it had been possible not to know about the existence of America. It was nothing short of amazing, to those who knew with how much care the geographers of Antiquity and the Arab world had described the universe.[38] In the lands of the Catholic monarchy an interest in others rapidly became a requirement, almost a criterion, of civilization. Early in the seventeenth century a Spanish bishop on a pastoral visit to San Miguel Culiacan, a small remote Mexican town near the Pacific coast, could scarcely restrain his sarcasm:

> The people of this small town can be compared to the first family formed by Adam and his children, because they do not think and do not understand that there might be other people than them in the world, and this is why they still dress as they did in the days of Nuño de Guzmán and his men; they are completely indifferent to receiving news or knowing if there is war or peace in the world or whether

the fleet is circulating normally; no one uses paper in the village, except for the notary.[39]

San Miguel was certainly 'a little frequented place to which no strangers went', and its isolation was largely to be explained by the distances which impeded commercial contacts; the poverty which was the result seemed more like a punishment for being closed in on itself than a consequence of economic facts: 'They do not think and do not understand that there might be other people than them in the world.' For the Spanish bishop, this ignorance and backwardness bordered on the sinful. By contrast, the elites of the capital rejoiced that Mexico City had become a centre of global exchanges and they sang the praises of communication between people and between societies.[40] On the other side of the world, the Portuguese of Goa manifested the same sentiment of being on the balcony of the world, and the same desire to lose nothing of the spectacle.

Modernity and Modernities

These reactions bring us face to face with forms of modernity which deviate from the canonical modernity claimed by western Europe. Far from France, far from Holland, from England and from Germany, other experiences became possible on the fringes of Iberian domination. Part of a history which could not but be 'global and conjunctural',[41] these modernities were formed in contact with other humanities and other bodies of knowledge, at the cost of immeasurable risks, unexpected exchanges and unprecedented acts of aggression.[42] They promoted the idea that there was nothing to prevent, nor should there be anything to prevent, communication between people. They assumed that every human being had the right to circulate and to settle anywhere he wished, in accord with the rights of peoples and natural law.[43] Morally, legally and philosophically, the great Iberian universities took on

the task of giving this their 'green light'. Yes, no impass-
able barrier separated Europe from the other worlds. Yes,
the torrid zone was perfectly habitable, contrary to what
the Ancients had believed and written. Yes, the non-
Christian societies which comprised – however deplorably
– the majority of humanity were certainly political societies with which one could do business, notwithstanding
differences of religion and of political and social organization. The deep conviction that there existed a universal
natural law proved that communication between worlds
was everywhere possible, even desirable.

The fact that these principles were constantly contra-
vened by the Iberians, who thought only of interpreting
them to their own benefit, does not detract from their
modernity. The feeling of spiritual and material responsibility, often sustained by a global optimism, simply
strengthened the Iberians, and then other Europeans, in
the conviction that not only ought they to intervene in the
fate of the rest of humanity, but that they had been chosen
for this. The educated Portuguese, in particular, cultivated
the theme of the providential choice of the people to whom
they belonged; for better and for worse.

The desire to know as it was expressed remote from
Europe was very far from being mere intellectual speculation. It was tried and tested in contact with other worlds,
against them and with them. It was the physical, human and
material collision with the great Amerindian and Asiatic
civilizations, as much as the debates in sixteenth-century
Spain on the nature of the newly discovered societies, that
put them at the forefront of European concerns. Aristotelianism provided the means to think the social and the political in any part of the world and to classify all human
societies. In the present, on the ground, the Iberians and
their hosts got to know each other in every sense of the
word. Everywhere, people learned to size each other up and
to appreciate – or detest – each other. They destroyed
anyone who resisted or they negotiated, if they had to; that
was often the rule in Africa, even more so in Asia.

We need to be careful not to extend to the world as a whole the shadow of the conquistador who razed everything in his path. Invaders in America, to which they brought devastating epidemics, in Asia the Iberians were outsiders, that is, when they did not die of a fever on the coasts of Africa or drown in one of the innumerable shipwrecks on the various oceans of the world. Colonists, missionaries, administrators, trading partners, artists or renegades who had fled to other worlds, Europeans became familiar with the presence of others: Indians of Mexico and the Andes, slaves and aristocrats of Africa, Brahmins and Muslims of India, Chinese pirates, Japanese samurai, mulattos and mestizos of every origin and every colour. The practical experience, with all its dangers and its daily might-have-beens, added to the mountains of information amassed locally, inspired a considerable number of texts, not all of which were the work of Europeans. Of course, those who made it or those who came to grief in these peripheral regions were infinitely more numerous than the writings which enable us to imagine them. Of most of them, the historian finds no trace.

The Monopoly of the Gaze?

It was certainly the Europeans of the sixteenth century who were in the forefront in establishing contacts with and making incursions into every part of the world, and also in giving these parts global visibility. The atlas of Abraham Ortelius, the *Theatrum Orbis Terrarum* (*Theatre of the World*) was a European invention but it was also a representation of the world which was read not only in America but also in China and Japan.

Nothing comparable was produced anywhere else in the world. When the Turks looked at America in the sixteenth century, it was through the prism of Italian translations, seemingly without ever attempting any investigation on the ground. When, early in the seventeenth century, the Mughal chronicler Tahir Muhammad wrote about Portugal, his information about Europe was sketchy and he even confused Portugal in general with the city of Lisbon.[44] Were these blunders a result of second-hand documentation or a lack of curiosity? It was easier, it may be argued, for a Christian to travel in Islamic or pagan lands than for a Muslim to live among the Infidel.[45] But the Chinese and Japanese, too, only rarely travelled to America or Europe. Although some Japanese, merchants and ambassadors, set foot in New Spain and in Europe, and some Chinese visited Mexico City and Lima, none of them went on to produce striking descriptions. The account of the Japanese embassy which travelled across Catholic Europe was in reality an initiative of the Society of Jesus, and the latter's influence is visible on every page written by these young Japanese.[46]

However, we should not underestimate the importance of this circulation of people, things and ideas simply because it was exceptional. Some mestizos from Spanish America visited Europe, leaving work of the first order; one need think only of the *Rhetorica christiana* of Diego Valadés, or the works of the Inca Garcilaso de la Vega.[47] Indians from America, like Domingo Chimalpahin and Guaman Poma de Ayala, were interested in the history of Europe and the history of the world. The attention paid by the *daimyo* of Japan to mannerist painting and European cartography is demonstrated by the sumptuous screens they commissioned to decorate their homes. Their curiosity about Mexico and the New World is now well known. At the beginning of the seventeenth century the court of the Great Mughal showed such a keen interest in the engravings of Dürer that it has been claimed as a 'revival' of the great German painter on Indian soil.[48] We may be confident that an exploration of the Turkish, Persian and Asian archives would add further examples and enable us to gain a better idea of the scale of extra-European travel, in particular by those who, outside the Catholic monarchy, invigorated the spaces of Islam in Africa and Asia, that is, a good half of the world.

Thinking the World

To be curious about others – 'What time is it there?' – is already to think the world; and to think the world no longer as an abstract sphere, largely unknown and imaginary, but as a globe – 'a perfect globe or ball . . . that has its boundaries and limits, its roundness and its vastness' –[49] populated by large numbers of people and societies to which it was now possible to have access. This was a first revolution. To become aware of the diversity of the peoples encountered, one after the other, and of the links of every kind, not only commercial or colonial, that were beginning to proliferate between continents was a second. The challenge was unprecedented. In the four quarters of the globe, men, women, societies, beliefs, fauna and flora came suddenly and violently into contact. 'History began to develop as an organic whole and events, as in a piece of woven fabric, to intertwine one with the other.'[50] The historian Polybius had had a premonition of this process of globalization, faced with the unification of the Roman world. Now it took concrete form in the mental, physical and existential revolution which spread in the sixteenth century as a consequence of European expansion. New approaches to the world needed to be devised in order to transform this maelstrom of impressions and information into something thinkable and alterable as the encounters and discoveries progressed. How to encompass in a single gaze the contacts that were being generalized between the four quarters of the globe,[51] now that, for the first time, Africa communicated with America, and America with Asia? How to interpret this global dynamic, unprecedented for Europeans but equally disconcerting for Muslims accustomed to contemplating other horizons? In both Istanbul and Mexico City – centres or peripheries? – people struggled to find answers to these questions.[52]

− 3 −

The International of
the Cosmographers

Say: 'Are they equal – those who know and those who
know not?'
Koran, Sura 39, verse 12, quoted in the *Tarih-i Hind-i
garbi*, p. 73

On the surface, everything separated the two cities: distance, the past, religion, geopolitics . . . Istanbul ruled one
of the greatest powers on earth, the Ottoman Empire;
Mexico City was only the capital of an American kingdom
attached to the Crown of Castile. The Turks had inherited
from Byzantium and the Roman Empire a thousand-year-
long past; the inhabitants of New Spain were constructing
a new world. The former were Muslims, imbued with their
role at the heart of Islam, the latter Christians, proud of
being in the vanguard of the Christianization of the world.
In short, histories with little in common were unfolding in
these two parts of the world. Is it possible that, nevertheless, the scholars of these two cities shared certain mental
viewpoints? Had the unification of the world advanced far
enough for the same structures of thought to prevail in
Istanbul and in Mexico City?

King's Cosmographer and Sultan's Astronomer

The references scattered throughout the *Tarih-i Hind-i garbi*, and the more reasonable of its hypotheses, show the Anonymous Chronicler of Istanbul to have been a cosmographer and an astronomer well-informed about the things of his day. He was as familiar with the great Christian texts on America as with Arabic and Persian science or the learning of Antiquity. Should this surprise us? In the second half of the fifteenth century, soon after the capture of the city, the sultan Mehmed II (1444–81) had set out to attract scholars from the Muslim world to the capital of his empire. In 1471 he summoned from Samarkand the great astronomer Ali Qushji, who brought his voluminous library with him to Istanbul.[1] Situated at the crossroads of Europe and Asia, the city was well placed to capitalize on the scholarship of the Arabs, the Persians and the Christians. Nor was this at the expense of the legacy of Antiquity. The work of Ptolemy was debated and retranslated, his maps were rediscovered and others procured from Italy, if they were not graciously presented by their authors. Great works of history were written. In short, the shores of the Bosphorus proved singularly favourable to cosmographical thinking and to historical research. A passage from the prologue of our Ottoman chronicler evokes this climate of intellectual activity: 'It was for a long time and a lengthy period, that, being safe from the merciless hands of difficult times and free from their painful grip, I have spent the ready cash of life and capital of health on objects of learning, knowledge, and beautiful sciences.' While we can reasonably guess what were the stages in the education of our anonymous writer in the capital of Suleiman the Magnificent, we remain in total ignorance as to what prompted him, unlike his peers, to take an interest in America and to assemble 'responsible truthful books and recent maps'.[2] It was not the desire to recover the heritage of the first Turkish experts on America, as he neither cites nor draws on them. Religious motives cannot be ruled out, but one wonders whether they are enough to account for his fixation on the 'New India', for his acute awareness of its implications for the world scene, for his love of knowledge, even if it was Christian in origin, or, last but not least, for a critical spirit which did not hesitate to contradict the very greatest.

We feel more comfortable, on the other hand, with Heinrich Martin.[3] In Mexico he bore the title of Cosmographer Royal. The Crown of Castile had instituted this post in order to keep the Council of the Indies informed about 'the lands and provinces, voyages and routes which should be followed by our galleons, our fleets and our vessels as they come and go'.[4] It was the job of the cosmographer to study the eclipses and movements of the stars, and he was also to measure the latitude and the longitude 'of the lands, towns, villages, rivers and mountains'. He was required to teach mathematics by developing a three-year programme: after a first year devoted to discussion of *The Sphere* of Johannes de Sacrobosco and to study of the *Theories of the Planets* of Georg von Peurbach,[5] the second year was spent teaching the first six books of Euclid and Ptolemy's *Almagest*; the syllabus for the third year included subjects relating to cosmography and navigation, and also the use of the astrolabe. By the second half of the sixteenth century all this knowledge was accessible in Mexico City, in the cloisters of the mendicant orders, at the university or among the Jesuits. There were many libraries giving the literate public access to the texts that were imported by printers and booksellers, including the *Revolutions of the Heavenly Spheres* of Copernicus.[6] Added to which were the productions of the capital's own presses. In 1557 the Augustine Alonso de la Veracruz published his *Physica speculatio*, which repeated the essentials of the astronomy and cosmology of Aristotle and Ptolemy without totally neglecting the contribution of Copernicus.[7] A manual of arithmetic was published in

Mexico in 1556, followed in 1587 by an introductory work on cosmography and astronomy.[8] Each of these, it is hardly necessary to add, were the first of their type in the continent of America.

Heinrich Martin was not the first cosmographer to set foot in New Spain. The Spanish Crown had already, on several previous occasions, shown its desire to add to knowledge in the new lands by despatching experts across the Atlantic. A Portuguese cosmographer, originally from Viana, Francisco Domínguez de Ocampo, had assisted the physician Francisco Hernández in the botanical and zoological work the latter carried out between 1570 and 1577. In the early 1580s dozens of *Relaciones Geográficas* recorded innumerable facts about the physical geography, natural history and physical and human resources of New Spain and Peru. In 1584, about five years before Heinrich Martin's arrival, a scientific mission observed an eclipse of the moon in Mexico City; the observation was led by a cosmographer from Valencia, Jaime Juan, and the Royal Armourer, Cristóbal Gudiel. They were assisted by the Portuguese Domínguez de Ocampo. Martin thus joined a scientific milieu which had already accumulated considerable experience of American realities.

Once settled in Mexico City, Heinrich Martin followed the progress of the colonization of the north of the continent, which constituted a mass of hitherto unknown lands which might conceal untold wealth. It is not known if he participated in the expedition of Juan de Oñate, which set out in 1598 to found a settlement in the kingdom of Quivira, but it was probably Martin who drew up one of the first maps of New Mexico.[9] The Pacific Ocean – the 'South Sea' – was also a tempting prospect, with its coasts generally safe from the incursions of European rivals. In 1602 Sebastián Vizcaíno was given the task of exploring the coasts of California at the head of an expedition of colonization, coupled with a scientific mission consisting of two cartographers and a cosmographer. The voyage was successful and, back in Mexico, Martin's services were again called on. He reproduced the thirty-two maps of the Pacific coast of Mexico, from Navidad to Cape Mendocino, drawn up by the cosmographer Gerónimo Martín Palacios (November 1603).[10] He was thus closely involved in the big questions for the geography of this part of the world: the colonization of what became the South of the United States, the reconnaissance of the coasts of North West America and the search for a passage to Asia – that mysterious Strait of Anian which fascinated all European cosmographers. Already familiar with the lands of Northern Europe and the Iberian Peninsula, Martin also acquired a good working knowledge of North America.

A Cosmography in Common

Both our cosmographers, the nomadic Heinrich Martin and the more sedentary Anonymous Chronicler, swore only by Ptolemy. In Mexico City and Istanbul alike, shortly before the year 1000 of the hegira and shortly after the year 1600, it was impossible to think the world outside an overall framework, a 'scientific' approach, that continued to be provided by the cosmography and astronomy of Antiquity. It should never be forgotten that Christendom and the Islamic lands shared a tradition stretching back more than a thousand years.

The educated classes of Mexico City and Istanbul had inherited the same ancient scholarship, often transmitted to Latin Christendom by the wise men of al-Andalus, Byzantium or the Near East. There was, as a result, a constant echo effect between Istanbul and Mexico City and a consensus that is ultimately hardly surprising. Let us listen to the Anonymous Chronicler: according to 'the masters of astronomy and the philosophers', the universe is composed of a group of spheres contained one inside the other, 'like the sheets of words' in a book. The ninth sphere, 'the greatest and finest and most famous' is the 'Sphere of Atlas, which in the language of the sharia [that

is, in Arabic] is called "arsh" . . . it is the highest heaven
and the determinant of times and seasons. It has the handle
of sovereignty and the hand of power over the other
spheres.' Below it is the 'ethereal space' of the, the 'Eighth
Heaven', which 'is ornamented and embellished by the
stationary stars and . . . twelve constellations';[11] or, as
Heinrich Martin put it, in Mexico, 'it is there that are
found the multitude of fixed stars'.[12] The German in
Mexico City and the Anonymous Chronicler in Istanbul
then both proceed to list the different spheres up to the
last one, the one corresponding to the Earth, which they
both made the centre of the universe. In Mexico City as
in Istanbul, geocentrism ruled.

The ancient tradition also validated a 'scientific' discourse constructed round the theory of the four elements:
fire, air, water and earth. From this theory derived a system
for interpreting the celestial and natural phenomena which
affected the last sphere, our earth, composed, as everyone
knew, of earth and water. They were agreed, too, on the
fact that the Earth was round. Both Heinrich Martin and
the Anonymous Chronicler believed this, which explained
why a traveller, if he moved from west to east, or from
east to west, would be sure to arrive back at his starting
point. It was also because the Earth was a globe that the
Anonymous Chronicler imagined a tunnel which would
lead to the antipodes of our world: 'Supposing that a direct
hole occur in the area of Andalusia, it would come out in
the area of Sin [China].'[13] The earth, lastly, was an entity
which could be measured and divided, which had a North
Pole and a South Pole and which was shared between two
hemispheres separated by an equator.[14] It was known how
to calculate its diameter and its circumference. By determ-
ining latitude and longitude, it was even possible accurately to locate any point on the globe, 'and the relationship
of every land to another is distinct and evident'.[15]

In other words, to describe the 'machine of the world',
Heinrich Martin and his eastern counterpart employed
the same age-old language and tools bequeathed by the

scholars of Antiquity. However, for the Anonymous Chronicler of Istanbul – who cites al-Masûdi, one of the most prestigious historians and geographers of the Arab world – this scholarship went back even beyond the Greeks, since it was in India (Hind) that the sky and the constellations had first been described.[16] In fact this community of views is less surprising than the fact that the ideas of Antiquity had gained a foothold in a new continent, following the expansion that had started with the Greeks and the Romans. The spread of Iberian globalization came about through the spread of a representation of the world that had come from the East and Antiquity before its active transmission by Arabic science.

'Fresh News'

This ancient scholarship was not without presenting some problems: how was knowledge of pagan origin (Aristotle, Alexander, Ptolemy) to be reconciled with the sacred facts in the Bible and the Koran? One can understand why, when Heinrich Martin quoted Aristotle and Plato to explain their ideas about the creation of the world, he felt obliged immediately to refute them by contrasting them with the Scriptures. But the real difficulty lay elsewhere. How was it possible not to take account of the discoveries of the sixteenth century, which challenged a whole series of assertions long regarded as unassailable? The exploration of the antipodes had demonstrated the limitations of ancient learning, including that of the Fathers of the Church, who had denied all possibility of life in the southern hemisphere or the torrid zone. But the old ideas died hard. They were still being debated at the end of the sixteenth century, in spite of the irrefutable evidence reported by thousands of travellers for over a hundred years. Heinrich Martin found it necessary to cross swords with one of his contemporaries and the Anonymous Chronicler was obliged to recall a few obvious truths: not only was the torrid zone inhabited but, to the south of it, there had been discovered – for which we should read 'Christians had discovered' – cold zones subject to the rigours of winter.

The task of the Anonymous Chronicler was made all the more difficult by the fact that the amalgam of ancient learning and Arabic and Persian science had gone so far that any questioning of the tradition reflected on the credibility of the scholars of Islam; especially when the 'fresh news' came from Christendom. For, rather than refer to the Ptolemy of the *Geographia*, he cited a cohort of Arab and Persian scholars who had greatly influenced the transmission of ancient knowledge and scientific thinking between the eleventh and the fifteenth centuries, that is, all 'those who were versed in astronomy and those who were of superior wisdom'. They included al-Masûdi of Baghdad, a geographer and historian (died 956), 'bearer of an ancient and providentialist tradition of history',[17] the Persian astronomer Nasir al-Tusi, the Persian cosmographer al-Kaswini (died 1283), Mawlana Nizam and the Arab scholar Ibn al-Wardi (died 1457), and in addition 'the sages of India'.[18] Not only did the Hispano-Portuguese discoveries lead him to contradict all these authors, but he was obliged to say that their knowledge of the old world, too, left much to be desired. This explains the wealth of precautions with which he surrounded himself – 'the humble writer ventures that . . .', 'the humble writer proposes that . . .' – when he had to signal or correct dubious, even erroneous, information.

Nevertheless, all sorts of fables and clichés still impeded his vision. By his telling, the island of Thule was the last inhabited region to the north; the most northerly tribes were distinguished by their bestiality, stupidity and lasciviousness; the island of Sarandusa (?Ceylon) abounded in gold to the point where all the tools and objects were forged from this precious metal; in the seas of India and China and the Persian Gulf there were gigantic whirlpools which swallowed up ships lured into their vicinity; the Antichrist lived, imprisoned on an island in the China Sea, and so on. On the other hand, he did not hesitate to challenge other, equally fabulous anecdotes reported by Arab and Persian authors, 'masters of composition and compilation'. And he made many criticisms of his predecessors. Even 'the Herodotus of the Arabs' did not escape: 'al-Masûdi who, among the historians, is admitted by all as a master in the science of disputation, is not aware of the truth of the situation and errs in a number of books'. The prestigious Ibn al-Wardi fared little better: 'It is true that the strange mistakes of the author of the *Kharidât al-'adja'ib* exceed all bounds and the shape [map] that he placed in the front of his book is beyond the realm of truth'.[19] No, the Crimean Sea was not linked to the Atlantic, nor did the Baltic Sea communicate with the Bosphorus, any more than the North Sea should be confused with the Sea of Azov, and so on.

The Anonymous Chronicler's criticism of the authorities became even more systematic when he tackled the question of the New World. 'The ancients of the ulema', that is, the interpreters of Islamic law, had believed that the Ocean had 'no limits to its boundaries, and Ptolemy, before them, had said that its limits were unknown. If the Pillars of Hercules had been built on the borders of the Mediterranean, it was to remind humans that it was impossible to voyage any further on this 'sea of darkness'.[20] Such ignorance was all the more embarrassing in that it had been the Christians who had been the first to tell the truth and benefit from it in the spread of their faith and the expansion of their trade. Hence the necessity of advancing a series of counter-facts designed to detract from the total novelty of the discovery of America. A certain Khashkhash had sailed the Ocean before returning to Andalusia with 'great loot' and relating strange tales;[21] at the beginning of the ninth century of the hegira (that is, the fifteenth century), men from Andalusia had reached the limit of the 'limitless sea';[22] lastly, it was not impossible that, in the time of Alexander the Great, Greeks had encountered a ship coming from the New World. Were these few reminders enough? They did not, in any case, prevent him from presenting the 'New India' as faithfully as he could, on the basis of exclusively Christian information.[23]

Our cosmographers were agreed on another point. Whatever criticisms they made of their predecessors or of generally held beliefs, they both, the Christian as well as the Muslim, were careful to locate their cosmography within an impeccably orthodox religious context, recalling, for example, that it was God who had created the world (Heinrich Martin) or that the last sphere was the seat of God (the Anonymous Chronicler). The new information gathered on America had to corroborate 'the wisdom of the Koranic verses', and the Holy Scriptures of the Christians could not be shown to be incorrect. The Inquisition in Mexico was as implacable as the guardians of the sharia in Istanbul. Should we be surprised that, in their vision of America, the two authors were alike in rejecting indigenous paganism, idolatry and cannibalism? This similarity of view was accompanied, even in the Anonymous Chronicler, by a few involuntary slips. Despite all his precautions, he occasionally used the Christian calendar without converting it into Islamic reckoning.[24] One can understand why he preferred to retain a prudent anonymity.

The Seven Climes of the Globe . . .

'It was extracted from Abdet ibn Abi Lubaba that the world is seven climes.'[25] In fact behind the Muslim scholar, who died in 741, lie concealed the ideas of the Alexandrian geographer Claudius Ptolemy, who had divided the world into seven thermal or climatic zones. The Anonymous Chronicler listed seven climes which formed seven zones parallel to the Equator, within each of which the length of the longest day varied by no more than half an hour to an hour.[26] These divisions, which also appear on the European mappa mundis of the Renaissance, cover only a

portion of the globe, stretching from China and the Far
East to the Atlantic Ocean. We find here the classic *oikoumene*, extending towards the Orient in line with the rate
of advance of Islam. The 'city of Muhammad' (Medina),
Mecca and 'Africa' (Tunisia) were located in the second
clime. The third included Kabul, Baghdad, Damascus,
Jerusalem, Alexandria, Cairo, Tripoli and Fez. In the
fourth were regions extending from Tibet and Khorasan
to Cordova, Spain and southern Andalusia. The town of
Valencia and eastern Andalusia belonged to the fifth clime,
together with the legendary and frightening 'lands of Gog'.
The lands of the Franks, Bulgaria and Constantinople
appeared in the sixth clime – at least in principle, because
the author certainly intended to correct the position of
Istanbul, 'the center of the throne of the Ottoman state',
which, according to his calculations, was rather situated
somewhere in the middle of the fifth clime.[27]

There was no division into continents, nor a dominant
continent, but a knowledge focused on the eastern Mediterranean and the Near East. Nor was there ethnocentrism, in the sense that neither Istanbul, 'place of prosperity
and place of the throne of the sultanate', nor the Ottoman
Empire appear as privileged cities or regions; rather there
was a real or virtual Islamocentrism. If the Anonymous
Chronicler remained generally faithful to Ptolemy (the
Geographia) and his Arab interpreters (al-Masûdi), his
conception of the world also had the advantage of conforming to an Islam practised from the Atlantic coast to
the Far East. He thus shared a world view already seven
centuries old. Had an Arab author not already, in the
eleventh century, in an anonymous account of China and
India, claimed that the world had four kings: the caliph,
the emperor of China, the king of India and the emperor
of Byzantium?[28] The Islamocentrism of our Anonymous
Chronicler even introduced a certain bitterness, so much
greater does his interest in the lands lost to the benefit of
Christendom seem than in those in which Islam reigned
supreme. The passages devoted to the beauty of Sicily, an

ancient Islamic land ignominiously fallen into the hands of the Infidel, speak for themselves.[29] After its conquest by the Muslims, it had become 'a center of the people of belief', but its loss had now delivered it into 'the darkness of unbelief and ignorance'. The fall of the kingdom of Granada was equally distressing to our author, who was careful to mention the underground resistance of the Muslims to Christianity in the Andalusian lands: 'While residing underground, thousands of pious and devout folk pray and worship with calls to prayer there. With sad heart and tearful experience they raise prayerful hands to God that from the commander of Islam a man of action may raise a banner of endeavor and resolution.' We should remember that the expulsion of the Moriscos from Spain, already being talked about in 1580, was still to come. The beauty of the mosque of Cordova, which he described at great length, provoked both nostalgia and anger in our author: 'It is not fitting that holy places of worship and fine mosques like this be churches or that the graves of the pious and the mansions of the ulema be filled with refuse.'[30] As for the non-Muslim world, it is only hinted at in his work, through the India beyond the Indian Ocean,[31] China or, even more distant, northern Europe.

The opening-up of America toppled this world order. The reader senses that the Anonymous Chronicler struggled to integrate the 'New India' into the Ancient world and the Ptolemaic and Muslim *oikoumene*; no doubt because all the threads which attached it to Europe, Africa and Asia were in Christian hands. Was he, nevertheless, a pioneer in this field? Everything suggests the contrary, and that Turkish circles had kept a watchful eye on the progress of the Great Discoveries since the beginning of the sixteenth century and been well able to obtain accurate information. The admiral Piri Reis managed to procure a map of Christopher Columbus dating from 1498, showing that the traffic in information about the Great Discoveries was not confined to Italian espionage in Lisbon and Seville. Piri Reis was also a cartographer and an acute observer.

His map of the world contained the first Turkish observations on the new continent, and his compendium for navigation, the *Kitab-i Bahriye* (1521),[32] many times copied,
included information about the American lands. In fact the
Anonymous Chronicler seems not to have used it or even
been aware of its existence. Other Turkish sources were
interested in America. One example from the middle of
the century (1554) is a work devoted to the Ocean (*al-
Muhit*), which fleshes out its presentation of the Red Sea
and the Indian Ocean with reflections on the New World,
the land of Magellan (*Magellanica*) and the Pacific. This
compilation is also owed to an admiral of the Ottoman
fleet, Seyyidi 'Ali Reis.[33]

There were many Europeans in Istanbul and the
Ottoman Empire, Christians, Jews or renegades converted
to Islam, who were able to supply news of Iberian expansion, provide maps and reports and introduce plants and
objects. The admiral Seyyidi 'Ali Reis claimed to have got
his information from a Portuguese captain who had circumnavigated the globe. It was a Hungarian renegade by
the name of Ali Macar Reis who, in 1567, compiled a map
of the world which is today preserved in Istanbul.[34] It
is even possible that Antonio Pigafetta, the chronicler
of Magellan, ended his days on the shores of the
Bosphorus.[35]

Seen from Istanbul, the America that was called the
'New India' lay between the Western Ocean and the
Eastern Ocean. It was divided into two parts: the lands of
the North or Yeni Ispanya (New Spain) and the lands of
the South (Peru). The northern part of the continent was
still unknown, but, according to the Anonymous Chronicler, its western coasts joined the lands of Çin and Macin,
that is, China. This is also what was believed and written
by the Christian geographers of the period. The South was
completely taken up by Spanish Peru to the detriment of
Brazil, reduced to the strict minimum, 'a town named
Brazil that is subject to the Portuguese';[36] was this proof
of the insidious influence of the Spanish gaze, disinclined

to take any notice of Portuguese America, or did it reflect a presence that was much more discreet than in the Indian Ocean?

. . . Or the Four Quarters of the Globe?

Like the *Tarih-i Hind-i garbi*, the *Repertorio* aimed to provide a general overview of the newly discovered lands. But here our German diverged from Ptolemy and his Muslim homologue. Succinctly, and in a way that became the norm in his day, he divided the planet into four parts, corresponding to Europe, Asia, Africa and America.[37] For Heinrich Martin it was self-evident that Europe was the principal part of the world; and Europe extended from Poland and Hungary to Spain and England, 'although it is an island'.[38] Asia, 'so famous among the authors', was only the second part of the world. Yet it might have claimed primacy on more than one count. Had it not been home to the first man, Adam, and the first great monarchies of the world, Assyrian, Persian and Medean? Our Lord had lived and died there on the cross; the Bible had been written there and it was on this continent that the Holy Places were found. The Asia of Heinrich Martin began with Muscovy, where Boris Godunov had recently died (1605), as if his journey to distant Courland (Latvia) had led him to push the land of Russia out of Europe.[39] The Tartar, the Turk and the Persian dominated this part of the world, with the exception of Portuguese Asia (*Asia de Portugal*) and 'Great China'. There is nothing, however, on the empire of the Great Mughal, although it was ruled at this period by the all-powerful Akbar. Africa appeared as the third part of the world. It included several vast regions: Barbary, Numidia, Libya and the 'Land of the Blacks', which extended from Cape Verde to the Cape of Good Hope.[40] A fifth region, Egypt, contained 'the great city of Cairo, in the old days called Babylon, [which] counts among the largest in the world',[41] but it was also the 'land of the Moors'. On the borders of this Islamic country, in the centre of Africa, in the kingdom of Nubia, lived the king of the Abyssinians, 'commonly called Prester John'; Martin remained faithful to an ancient tradition which placed this part of Africa under the rule of the legendary king.

The fourth part of the world, unknown to the Ancients, was easily distinguished from the other three because it was separated from them by the waters of the Ocean: this was the 'New World' (Heinrich Martin did not use the word America). It measured nearly 2,200 leagues from north to south and 1,300 leagues from east to west. It was not the least blessed part of the world, far from it: '[It] exceeds all the others in size and riches'. It was the jewel of the Spanish monarchy, which had 'two vast kingdoms' there, Peru and New Spain. And there was no way he was going to talk about this new world without referring to the mystery of the origin of its inhabitants, a subject on which much ink had already been spilled on both sides of the Atlantic. If, after the Flood, humans had spread all over the planet, moving from Asia to Europe and Africa, how had they been able to reach America? Martin had no intention of being left out of the debate. He rejected an arrival by sea or by air; rather he inclined to the idea of a population of Asian origin that had arrived by a land route, via the Strait of Anian, to the north of the Pacific Ocean.[42] This Asian hypothesis was to him all the more convincing in that, on his travels in Courland, as we have seen, he had encountered a population which resembled the Indians of New Spain – probably members of the community of Finnish origin which then populated the north of the country, and whose dialect differed from the Slav languages.

In any case, the Christian of Mexico City shared with the Muslim of Istanbul the conviction that, whatever or whoever they were, human beings had common origins and a common history. They neither of them invented anything and they drew on the scholarship of a thousand years to describe the world, the division into continents being no more 'modern' than the division into climes. Even though the continental model probably lent itself more easily to the addition of a 'fourth part' than the 'climatic' model, which supposed, if it was to be extended to the American lands, a deeper knowledge of the lands and latitudes of the New World.

– 4 –

Antwerp, Daughter
of Alexandria

The fundamental event of the modern age is the conquest
of the world as picture.
Martin Heidegger, *The Age of the World Picture*

In the sixteenth century one same image of the world prevailed from Istanbul to Mexico City. Formed on this side
of the Atlantic, it began to conquer the globe and it spread
to America, crucial stage in a process in which images
became increasingly standardized, and which culminated
in the twentieth century. It is at the end of this unstoppable
dynamic that now, all over the planet, we share a single
representation of the world, a representation which seems
to us both natural and scientific, but which is actually the
product of a construction and a conditioning that can
easily be traced. The expansion of western Europe owes
much to the formidable dynamism which drove its geographers to appropriate the globe intellectually, produce an
image of it and then impose this image on the rest of the
planet. It is one of the paths taken by European globalization in order to dictate to the rest of the planet ways of

seeing, of thinking and of calculating that were developed within the societies of Islam and Christendom.

The 'Prince of Geographers'

From Istanbul to Mexico City and from Manila to Goa, people conceived of the Earth and the universe in the manner of Aristotle and Ptolemy, and of the generations of scholars who had discussed and glossed them: Aristotle for the intellectual and cosmographical foundations, Claudius Ptolemy for the geographical science and the calculations, as if the *Geographia* of the Alexandrian scholar had been the 'geographical Bible' not only of the Christians of the Renaissance,[1] but also and even more of their Muslim neighbours. Whatever corrections their contemporaries made, and the existence of the New World was a major one, the 'prince of geographers' continued to loom large in the minds of cosmographers. Just like his Turkish counterpart, Heinrich Martin looked at the globe and the cosmos through Ptolemaic eyes; thus, when he recalled the miniscule speck the Earth constituted in the firmament, he quoted the fifth chapter of the first book of the *Almagest*.[2] And when the Anonymous Chronicler wondered about the circumference and the diameter of the globe, even the habitability of the Earth, it was to the *Almagest* that he, too, referred.[3]

What did Ptolemy represent for our two authors? Ptolemy the geographer left two major works, a treatise on astronomy, subsequently known by the name given to it by the Arabs, the *Almagest*, and a *Guide to Geography*, also known as the *Geographia* or *Cosmographia*. To compile his *Geographia*, this man of the second century drew on a considerable body of information, much of which came from the East. He used it to develop a powerful synthesis which leaped lightly over the centuries. Both Christians and Muslims drew on it for intellectual tools and essential notions, first and foremost the idea that the

Earth was a sphere and that it could be measured. Ptolemy shared this certainty with illustrious predecessors such as Aristotle, Pythagoras and Eratosthenes. He claimed to have established a more exact image of the globe, discarding myths and superstitions. He proposed a systematic and methodical approach to the representation of the world, tackling the difficulties raised by the portrayal in two dimensions of a spherical reality like the Earth. It was also Ptolemy who devised the first maps oriented to the North, the meridians and the scales.[4] He even seems to have compiled a mappa mundi, together with twenty-six other maps covering Europe, Africa and Asia. Practical geography and mathematical geography, a coming-together of arithmetic and imagination, a global vision: the work of Ptolemy envisages the Earth in its entirety.[5] In addition to which he was conscious of living within an *oikoumene* in the process of unification under the impact of Roman power. Ptolemy sought to think the world and provided himself with the means.[6]

Nevertheless, by the fifteenth century there was widespread awareness of the shortcomings of a scholar who had made a succession of errors in measurement and location. Many questions remained unanswered. What was the exact circumference of the Earth? Were the emerged lands entirely surrounded by water? Were the seas more extensive than the continents? In Istanbul the Anonymous Chronicler tried to get this point over. He knew that travellers who had visited the region of the sources of the Nile had not encountered the sea, but that the great extent of the oceans had allowed the 'ships-of-calamity of the evil-acting Portugal' to sail down the Atlantic, skirt round 'the Mountains of the Moon, which are the sources of the Nile' and arrive in the Indian Ocean.[7] With regard to many countries about which little was still known, Ptolemy had been silent. The Anonymous Chronicler wondered what the regions of north-west Europe were like, and what was known about the 'junction of the above-mentioned gulf [the Baltic] to the Eastern Ocean [the Pacific]'.[8]

The Ptolemy of the Arabs and the Ptolemy of Europe

But the Ptolemy of Mexico was no longer exactly the same as the Ptolemy of Istanbul. The considerable time lag which had for centuries been to the advantage of the scholars of Constantinople and Islam was reversed in the sixteenth century. Arabs and Byzantines had enjoyed easy access to the writings of Ptolemy for a long time. They had not only been able to save them from disappearance and oblivion, but they had put them to good use. It was thanks to this knowledge that the geographers al-Khwarismi and Ishaq ibn Hunaîn (809–73)[9] – the 'Ptolemy of the Arabs' – and the monk Maximus Planudes (c.1260–1310) had advanced Arabic and Byzantine science. But while the Muslim world had long made use of the *Geographia*, which had been translated into Arabic since the ninth century, the work remained unknown to Europeans. Until, that is, a Latin version became available in the Rome of the popes at the very beginning of the fifteenth century.[10] The time lost was soon made up. With the Bible, the *Geographia* was one of the first printed books and it was soon widely known,[11] benefiting from two major developments associated with the origins of the European Renaissance, the fall of the Byzantine Empire and the rise of printing.

The work of Ptolemy brought to an end the medieval representation of the world which had long predominated in western Europe. Fundamentally Christian and theological, it had expressed a religious interpretation far more than a geographical image. The Earth had appeared as a flat disk, on which three continents, Asia, Africa and Europe, composed an almost perfect T. At the centre, the city of Jerusalem had marked the absolute primacy of the reference to the Holy Scriptures: centre of the world and centre of History. The Ocean had surrounded all these emerged lands. This image died hard, in spite of the return of Ptolemy and the geographical facts made widely known by the Discoveries. It is paradoxical that this representation of the world even reached Mexico, where it appeared in the 1570s in the work of the indigenous artists who decorated the Florentine Codex; here, as if nothing had changed, the disk of the land, divided by a reversed T, continued to portray only the three parts of the Old World: an Earth without the New World and hence without either Mexico or Indians!

If the rediscovered work of the Alexandrian scholar became an essential point of reference for the Europeans of the Renaissance, it was because it offered 'a fuller, clearer window on to our world than any other available work'.[12] Ptolemy might err, but his errors did not in any way detract from the acuteness of his gaze or his methods. For fifteenth- and sixteenth-century readers the Ptolemaic view of the world was not only revolutionary but also reassuring and familiar. His vital axis, the Mediterranean, bathed the two peninsulas involved in the history of the Renaissance and of the Discoveries, Italy and Iberia. We might today be more inclined to think that the inadequacies and the errors of this way of presenting the world must have been an obstacle to the revisions made necessary by the constant stream of discoveries. In fact the opposite was the case. These shortcomings were a stimulus to a boundless curiosity and to an 'intense intellectual, many-sided and topical activity surrounding the dominant theme of the discoveries'.[13] The very greatest scholars had turned to Ptolemy. In 1578, when the *Tarih-i Hind-i garbi* was being written, the Flemish Gerardus Mercator published yet another edition of the *Geographia* before completing his own *Atlas sive cosmographicae meditationes*.[14] It was an act of homage by a great geographer to the scholar of Alexandria, whose maps were by then, in reality, only of retrospective historical interest.[15]

The Ptolemy of Flanders

In the sixteenth century the Spanish Low Countries and northern Europe became active centres of geographical thought and production. This explains why Heinrich Martin was not only interested in the Ptolemy of Alexandria. Like many of his contemporaries, he was also deeply indebted to the Ptolemy of Flanders. Like them, he had easy access to the *Theatrum* of Abraham Ortelius of Antwerp, who had himself wished to emulate the 'prince of geographers'.[16] From its first Antwerp edition, in 1570, the atlas of Ortelius was a huge success; King Philip II and Queen Elizabeth's minister William Cecil were among the assiduous readers of this remarkable work.

What might our German from Hamburg find there? The *Theatrum* marked a decisive turning point in the history of the representation of the globe. It was the first atlas. It was both an object and a tool, which have become familiar to us, but which surprised and enchanted its first users. It consisted of a single volume and it was easy to consult and to handle.[17] The format, which broke with the huge wall maps and heavy and cumbersome globes of the period, gave an unprecedented closeness to every part of the world. It has been described as a 'library without walls'. Ortelius explained that he had wanted to provide his readers with a 'shop' – we would say a geographical and bibliographical database without precedent – in which enthusiastic geographers could find everything they needed.[18] His *Theatrum* was an inventory of the world to be apprehended visually, through a set of conventions which presented the regions of the globe in the same fashion, always pleasing to the eye and orderly to the mind.[19] Like the Teatro Olimpico of Vicenza, it made it possible to see everything, to encompass everything, 'without moving'. The aesthetic harmony of the maps eschewed all reference to the conflicts which pitted kingdoms and religions against each other. People and countries coexisted on the planet, 'in this common house which the Creator has prepared for the community of mortals'.[20] By his choice of form, Ortelius had 'made the earth portable'.[21]

This unprecedented proximity could even give rise to a subtle empathy with the other civilizations of the planet, an empathy probably bound up with the deep convictions of the Antwerp scholar. One detects in the geographical construction and editorial enterprise of Ortelius traces of a religious sensibility peculiar to the southern Low Countries; or, to be more precise, to a milieu whose religious commitment and irenicism aspired to transcend the fracture between Reformation and Counter-Reformation in favour of a more peaceable view of the world. Reading the atlas was an encouragement to make more links and comparisons between peoples and spaces. It suggested possible associations, it sharpened the curiosity and it raised questions about the still unknown distant spaces; it even physically relativized the place of western Europe in the body of continents. There is no doubt that a work of this type made a major contribution to instilling in Europeans a sense of belonging to one same humanity and one same planet. As one turns over the pages, the finger and the eye move in an instant from one continent to another; it was an invitation to imagine, in the calm of one's study, other peoples, other countries and other ways of life. What time is it there?

It is an irony of history that, two years after the publication of the *Theatrum*, the Low Countries of Ortelius was engulfed in war between Spanish troops and Flemish rebels. We are reminded that showing the world was more than the pastime of a humanist imbued with irenicism. Merchants, soldiers and diplomats, too, wanted to be informed about the political map of the globe, to follow in an atlas the progress of the wars then ravaging Europe and to trace the commercial routes which united Europe to the rest of the world.[22] To which it should be added that the *Theatrum* was compiled by a subject of Philip II; it was dedicated to the 'king of the Indies and the Spains, monarch of the greatest empire of all times and of the whole earth', and Ortelius was rewarded with the title of 'Geographer Royal' (1573).[23] Was this atlas, ultimately, simply an instrument of propaganda in the service of the Catholic monarch?[24]

The understandable caution of Ortelius and his circle of friends means it is difficult to say. It would have been dangerous for them to confront Spanish power directly in a town which belonged to Philip II. On the other hand, while the *Theatrum* is not Hispanocentric, the point of view it overtly proclaims is European. The atlas was conceived and executed in Antwerp, not the Iberian Peninsula. With Ortelius, the gaze was both Europeanized and globalized. For the Antwerp observer it was Europe which led the world, not the Catholic monarchy.

The frontispiece of the *Theatrum*, an arch surmounted by a Europe in majesty, signals from the outset how Ortelius conceived the world. The harmony of the globe had its guide and its price. The allegorical engraving emphasizes the dominion of Europe over Africa, Asia and America. Beautiful Europe holds the 'rudder' of the world, which is in the form of a cross planted on the globe. Above her, bunches of grapes form a rustic arch, redolent with Christian and Antique references. A celestial globe and a terrestrial globe stand one on either side of this beautiful lady. She alone is seated – Africa and Asia stand below her, America slumps on the ground – and she alone looks directly at the reader. Naked and a man-hunter, America indulges her anthropophagous instincts,[25] brandishing in her left hand an obviously severed European head. Next to her is a bust symbolizing the 'land of Magellan', discovered by the navigator and soon restored to shadowy obscurity, prefiguration of a fifth part of the world of which all that remains today is Australia.

The Eurocentrism displayed by the frontispiece is also reflected in the amount of attention Ortelius devotes to the different parts of the world. While America merits only a single map, and Africa two, in the edition of 1570, with Asia rather better provided, with eight, there are forty maps covering Europe, country by country. Nevertheless, the smallness of Europe, which included Muscovy but excluded Asia Minor, is made plain by Ortelius. It is flanked to the east and to the south by Muslim or pagan countries. Only the seas opened doors for it to the world, and only the countries adjoining the Mediterranean and the Atlantic could project it beyond itself. Thus the geopolitics of Ortelius, as implied by his frontispiece, destine Europe to crush America and the fifth continent, leaving aside – for the time being – the lands of Africa and Asia.

The eye of Ortelius privileged Europe; and the best part and heart of the continent was in his eyes Brabant, his native land, and his town of Antwerp, 'situated upon the Scheldt, the most famous mart not only of "Germanie" but of all Europe . . . one of the strongest cities in the world . . . much beautified . . . scarcely to be matched in Europe'.[26] So Ortelius looked at the world from Antwerp, Brabant and Europe, and who would blame him? This anchoring seems inseparable from a remarkable openness to the world, because, as noted above, the atlas showed 'this common house which the Creator has prepared to shelter mortals'. In making the world a 'common house', the atlas of Ortelius marked the culmination of an extraordinary conditioning process of which we are today the heirs. It confined people in an image of the world, and humanity in a representation of the planet, which would come to seem the only ones possible and the most natural. One understands why, centuries later, Martin Heidegger associated the development of modernity with the conquest of the world 'as picture'.[27]

There is no reason to think that the cosmographer of Istanbul had access to the Antwerp atlas or had seen the map of the Turkish Empire it contained, even though he completed his manuscript a decade after the first edition of the *Theatrum*. Which is not to say that the Ottoman Empire was ignorant of European cartography; Istanbul could easily obtain maps through its favoured intermediary, Venice. In Mexico, Heinrich Martin had ample time to contemplate the image of the New World provided by the *Theatrum* of Ortelius. Ortelius included in the first edition a map of America inspired by that of Diego Gutierrez. A map of New Spain was added in 1579;

ten years later a new edition had a map of the Pacific, *Maris Pacifici*. The fact of living on the peripheries of the Catholic monarchy did not mean that one was left at the stage door of the 'Theatre', or even in its corridors. The inhabitants of Mexico and Europe all lodged in the 'house of the Father'; and the atlas was there to prove it.

The World from Mexico

It is a curious fact that the America presented by the atlas of Ortelius is very similar to that of the Anonymous Chronicler of Istanbul. What Ortelius reports about Mexico is essentially confined to episodes from the Spanish conquest: the campaigns of Hernán Cortés, the fall of Moctezuma's capital, the massacres of the indigenous population, a hint of Lascasianism, leavened with a large dose of exoticism before the term. In fact Ortelius was simply repeating the information that was circulating at that time in Europe and the Ottoman Empire. Both places seem to have been interested only in the pre-Hispanic worlds and the Indians of the Conquest, cannibals like the Brazilians and the Caribs or civilized like the Incas and the ancient Mexicans. Of Hispanic and colonial America, less strange and also less tragic, hence less interesting for the reader, and of the new societies that were being constructed, little emerges. In fact the Black Legend orchestrated by the enemies of Spain acted as an impediment to observation. It was as if evoking the cruelties of the Conquest exempted one from thinking about the future of the New World.[28] In this respect the *Repertorio* of Heinrich Martin offers a highly original point of view, as he shifts the focus of attention to what had happened after the conquest, that is, to a colonial society in gestation.

Let us see how he does this. First by changing the continent and the ocean of the viewpoint. In the *Repertorio* it is as if Mexico City has taken the place of Antwerp, and New Spain that of Brabant. Neither Hamburg nor his native Germany could serve as point of reference for Heinrich Martin. Anxious to adapt his observations to the place in which he found himself, he set out to determine 'to which celestial sign this New Spain is subject'.[29] And he asked the same question with regard to the 'heart of New Spain', Mexico City, described by Ortelius as 'royal city or, to put it better, queen of all the cities of the New World'.[30] According to the calculations of Heinrich Martin, the site of Mexico City was under the ascendant of Capricorn at the time of the creation of the world, and 'it seems that the planet which predominates in this kingdom is Venus with the participation of the Sun'. The position of New Spain had to be fixed as accurately as possible on the globe and in relation to the sky: 'The constellation which passes through the vertical of the whole of this region is the image of the horse Pegasus, which consists of twenty stars and extends from the equator to the Arctic North Pole from 7 to 25 degrees.'[31] The sky of New Spain was clearly not that of the distant European Spain. Martin was an astronomer; his scientific training meant he never lost sight of the fact that he was writing and making his calculations in Mexico City and Mexico. The country is approached from every angle: latitude, longitude, variations in the length of the day and the night – between 13 hours 9 minutes 36 seconds and 10 hours 54 minutes 24 seconds, regime of rains and tides, diagnostic epidemiology of the town of Mexico and climate.

On this last point, Heinrich Martin was driven to cross swords with a scholar, Blas Alvarez de Miraval, who, from his ivory tower in Salamanca, had published in 1599 *La Conservación de la salud del cuerpo y del alma*, in which he had the effrontery to claim that only the fifth part of the globe, the one lying between the Arctic North Pole and the Tropic of Cancer, was habitable. The southern hemisphere might perhaps be habitable, wrote the doctor of Salamanca, but whether it was actually populated was not known. The intermediary zone, according to him, called torrid, made any trade or communication between people impossible. The existence of Mexico City, Buenos Aires, Chile and Panama rendered such an assertion absurd, but it was still not without its supporters in late sixteenth-century Spain. It was easy for Martin to point out that, quite apart from New Spain, Peru and the India of Portugal, a large part of Persia, southern China, the Moluccas and the Philippines were all indubitably inhabited. And all these lands lay within the torrid zone, 'where many regions enjoy the mildest climate in the world'. In spelling this out, he had a dig in passing at one of the natural superiorities of the continent of Europe, its temperate climate.

Not content with such common-sense arguments, Martin also set out to demonstrate his analysis scientifically, by explaining that the mass of air was 'stronger' and colder 'inside the tropics than outside them'. He called on the 'Philosopher' – for whom we should read Aristotle – for assistance in explaining that it was the very quality of the tropical air which was the cause of the diversity of climates from which the torrid zone and New Spain in particular benefited. This diversity, far greater than that observed in Europe and Spain, meant that 'in only a small space' stifling valleys succeeded icy mountains. Not only was the torrid zone well populated, but the peoples who lived there were very varied, a logical reflection of the infinite diversity of the human race: 'It is natural that between thousands of persons, even if they are all born in the same country, you never find two who are exactly the same, in gesture, stature, colour and character'. In the New World, the Indians of New Spain were superior to those of the Caribbean Islands and Florida, the Blacks of Mexico were better than those of Guinea and the Iberian Peninsula; of course, the Spanish surpassed them all in capacity (*en habilidad*).[32]

To add further weight to his decentring, Martin calculated mathematically the tropical position of Mexico City, 'the most important town of this New World',[33] making its meridian a meridian of reference for the rest of the planet. He provided a table which gave the differences of longitude between Mexico City and a series of towns in America, Europe and Asia. The reader was able to discover the time differences which separated the capital of New Spain from all these other cities. Further, the table made it possible to calculate the eclipses of the sun and moon anywhere on the globe. This meant that a work conceived and published in Mexico could have a universal impact, a universality which confirmed the claims of the Catholic monarchy.

Even better than a map of the world, the table of Heinrich Martin confronted the reader with the planetary dimension of Spanish domination. While, for Ortelius, everything started from Antwerp and Europe, the viewpoint here is Mexican, and the list of cities of the world overwhelmingly American: Mexico is represented by 32 places, South and Central America by 35, including three in Brazil and five in the Caribbean, whereas a mere sixteen towns represent Spain and fewer than a dozen Asia. In this way Martin managed to specify a viewpoint which combined the local – the meridian of Mexico City – and the universal, while basing himself firmly in the American continent. This was a silent revolution in relation to the Eurocentric bias of the atlases and treatises of the Old World.

Decentring the Gaze

Heinrich Martin liked to emphasize the pioneering nature of his approach, and with good reason in the case of the geographical and strictly scientific dimensions of his thought. However, he was not alone among his contemporaries in striving to escape the European straitjacket. Others, too, thought the world by distancing themselves from the Eurocentrism or Hispanocentrism prevailing on the other side of the Atlantic. It was perfectly possible for an attachment to the Catholic monarchy to coexist with standpoints and claims which rejected the European image of an

America that was savage when it was not vanquished or subjected to the cruelties of the Spanish conquerors.

There are many explanations for this desire to valorize the American position. The wealth of the Indies, the pride of its new inhabitants and the consolidation of colonial society all encouraged a distancing with regard to the Old World. The maritime link established in 1566 between Manila and Acapulco had caused a repositioning of the Indies on the globe. It had both opened the doors of Asia to the inhabitants of New Spain and Peru and brought the East significantly closer to the coasts of New Spain. In *Grandeza mexicana* (1601) the poet Bernardo de Balbuena has striking phrases to express the exceptional position of Mexico City in the world. Nor is it surprising that one of the first works on the Philippines, Antonio de Morga's *Sucesos de Filipinas*, should be printed in Mexico in 1609. It could just as easily have been published in Spain, but it was in the capital of the New World that it appeared and it was aimed at a public which saw direct relations between this continent and the Philippines as the best way of counter-balancing colonial dependence.

Other representatives of the Crown managed to grasp the true position of New Spain in the world. Rodrigo de Vivero, a Spanish nobleman born in Mexico in the mid sixteenth century, combined attachment to Mexican soil with an impressive transoceanic vision. The Americanism of Vivero was sustained by the wealth of the New World; it was the silver of Mexico and Peru that made Spain stronger than France, England, Germany, Flanders and even the Great Turk. His planetary vision, which was made explicit when he spoke of 'this almost complete map of the world' that was held in his head, also extended to Asia and Japan. For Vivero, stronger economic links between the Japanese Archipelago and New Spain could only accelerate the expansion of his native town.[34]

The decentring of the gaze could have religious roots, too. The ambitions of the soldiers and the material interests of the merchants and great Creole families already pushed Mexico towards Asia, but the Franciscan Juan de Torquemada went further by incorporating this expansion into the great drive to Christianize the world which inspired the order of St Francis. His *Monarquía indiana*, published in Seville at the beginning of the seventeenth century, laid out a very much more ambitious programme than that of the *Sucesos de Filipinas*. It developed a Franciscan history of Mexico which, as the work progresses, ultimately acquires inter-continental proportions, extending to the whole Pacific area and reaching the coasts of China and Japan. Franciscans and Dominicans had already eulogized the role of America as cradle of a new Christendom, apparently saved from European heresies and established in the outposts of Asia. Torquemada consecrated this planetary projection.[35]

A Multiplicity of Points of View

The decentred gaze of Heinrich Martin and of the people of New Spain was by no means unique at that time. Just as it opened up unprecedented planetary horizons, Iberian globalization also gave rise everywhere to viewpoints that were irreconcilable with each other but complementary in their effort to grasp the global nature of the world. In the south Atlantic, commercial networks based on the slave trade constructed a 'Tropic of Capricorn' between Africa and Brazil, which had its own aims and strategies.[36] On the other side of Africa, facing the Indian Ocean, a vast missionary arc developed, which extended as far as Sumatra and which could be given the name 'Ethiopia Oriental', by reference to the great work devoted to this part of the world by the Portuguese Dominican João dos Santos – its counterpart for the American side of the globe being the *Monarquía indiana* of Torquemada. Around the Philippines and the Spice Islands there emerged a 'back of beyond' which became the focus of the ambitions of the merchants and missionaries who were eyeing the riches of

China, Korea and Japan. It was impossible to merge all these viewpoints into either the irenic Eurocentrism – or 'soft' imperialism – of an Abraham Ortelius or the more aggressive Hispanocentrism of the accredited chroniclers of the Iberian Empires. Although, even for an 'official' Portuguese historian like Diogo do Couto, the centre of the world tended to be identified with Goa rather than Lisbon. In Europe, the Eurocentrism in gestation was everywhere challenged by the local reference, an equally embryonic form of nationalism: the Anglocentrism of the England of John Dee, the Hispanocentrism of Madrid or even the Lusitanianism of Lisbon. France, meanwhile, proclaimed its own vision of the globe, even if it meant claiming only the third part of it, that of the southern mists, as it was still unknown, so still up for grabs.[37]

And there were other gazes, non-European, which learned, in their turn, to see the world in the way that was suggested to them by the Europeans: the educated Indians and mestizos of Mexico and Peru, subject to the Spanish Crown but proud of their past, or the Japanese lords who collected European maps and adorned their interiors with large multicoloured screens on which the plates from European atlases were displayed. The smallness of the Japan shown on the maps of 'the Barbarians of the South' had at first repelled this clientele, curious about European things, but it had not prevented the proliferation of the planisphere screens.

Back to Istanbul

The more the gaze became globalized in the sixteenth century, the more knowledge of the local deepened. Some chose Antwerp or Naples as vantage point from which to view Europe and the world, others settled on Mexico City so as to face Europe and Japan.

The Anonymous Chronicler of Istanbul, however, seems to have had some difficulty in developing his view of the world. Was this perhaps because he was unable to engage in this remarkable dialogue between the local and the global? Combining a critical loyalty to the traditional cosmography with an interest in 'fresh news', he still tried to embrace the world in its entirety. But did he succeed in showing more than a globe consisting of the juxtaposition of two eminently dissimilar parts, an Ancient World known since the Indians and the Greeks, largely dominated by Islam, and a pagan and Christian 'New India' which, sadly, could only be approached through the Christian chroniclers?

How could this other part of the world be integrated into the Islamic planet? A Muslim scholar, Idrîsî, had preceded him in a comparable task. In the middle of the twelfth century he had introduced Christian Europe into Muslim geography, in order to understand 'the world as a whole, without anything left out'.[38] By using geography to achieve an intellectual mastery of the world, by operating from a local base doubly defined as the Arabo-Christian Sicily of King Roger and the Mediterranean and by homogenizing his facts Idrîsî had gone as far as it was possible to go in the Middle Ages in achieving a global understanding of the planet. For the Anonymous Chronicler, however, it was not only Christian Europe that had to be integrated, but a whole new world which flew in the face of his scholarship.

The difficulty of the task only serves to emphasize his originality and his boldness. He did not hesitate to present himself as a pioneer in a milieu which was much more focused on the conquests of eastern Europe, the waters of the Mediterranean, the advances of Persia and even the shores of the Indian Ocean. Is it surprising that the Ottoman elites were less sensitive to the American developments of Iberian globalization and more interested in events in Islamic lands? *The Travels and Adventures* of the Turkish Admiral Seyyidi 'Ali Reis shows how this curiosity was directed towards regions within the Muslim sphere of influence.[39] With the acuteness of vision of a sailor and of a traveller who had crossed India and central Asia in the mid sixteenth century, Seyyidi 'Ali Reis offers his mirror of the world. With the exception of Vienna, which he wrongly describes as a possession of the sultan, Catholic Europe seems remote from his interests. His conversations with Mughal interlocutors, on the other hand, devoted to debating the extent of their respective empires and comparing them with that of Alexander the Great, reveal other horizons; and these horizons extended as far as China, since even there, they said in India, Turkish merchants invoked the name of the Ottoman sultan in their prayers.

This brings out with even greater clarity the originality of the *Tarih-i Hind-i garbi*, which demands both a restructuring and a reorientation of the gaze. There is no doubt that this shift was due to the advance of Iberian globalization, or, to be more precise, to a realization of the planetary dimension acquired by the empire of Philip II. It was this worrying reality that determined the reactions of the Anonymous Chronicler, whether in his determined search for Christian information about the world or in the construction of a body of knowledge as yet little cultivated in Turkey. But his motives were not only intellectual. He was also trying to respond to the extraordinary character of the discoveries and to the frustration that seems to have consumed him at feeling excluded from a part of the world, even irrevocably wrong-footed in this land that he called the New India.

– 5 –

Histories of the World and of the New World

In this year 1520, on 8 October, Fernand de Magellan
discovered and navigated the strait that bears his name.
    Heinrich Martin, *Repertorio de los tiempos*, p. 237

In the eyes of the Anonymous Chronicler, the discovery of
the 'New India', or, if preferred, its 'revelation' to the
Christians, was an event of huge importance: 'Since the
prophet Adam came into and set foot upon the world . . . up
to the present such a strange and wonderful matter has
never occurred or taken place.'[1]

These words recall those with which, thirty years earlier,
the chronicler Francisco López de Gómara had hailed the
discovery of America as the most important event in the
history of the world since the Incarnation. Yet, for a
Muslim, this unprecedented episode was inevitably a cause
for concern. Far from sharing the enthusiasm of the Spanish
chroniclers with whose writings he was familiar, the Anonymous Chronicler sent out a cry of alarm to believers,
stating three obvious facts: the Muslims had played no
part in this discovery and conquest; they had no direct
knowledge of America nor any influence on that continent;
they were 'without news' of what had happened there

since the Spanish conquest. The situation was all the more disquieting in that the Spanish and the Portuguese circulated freely between Europe and the New World, between Africa and China and between Mexico and the Philippines, as if no sea on the globe was outside their orbit.

A Turkish History of America

The Anonymous Chronicler drew his knowledge of America from several major European chronicles which had reached Turkey in Italian translations. He made use of only a handful of works, but they were all among the major sources published in Europe during the sixteenth century. They were largely the same as those then circulating in the Low Countries, hence at the heart of Christendom, and influencing the way in which people conceived of and spoke about America;[2] this says much for the quality of the selection made in Istanbul. The chronicles of Peter Martyr d'Anghiera, Gonzalo Fernández de Oviedo, Francisco López de Gómara and Agustín de Zarate provided the essential facts for his work and they were plagiarized in the manner customary in an age shameless in its practice of the art of 'cut and paste'.[3] The origin of the translations also reveals considerable familiarity with the *Navigationi et Viaggi* of the Venetian Ramusio, a collection of travel stories renowned in its day, published in 1550, frequently reprinted since and of crucial importance in the diffusion of information about the Iberian discoveries.[4]

In spite of the periodic confrontations between the Italian states and the Ottoman and Barbary states, exchanges between Islam and the Peninsula had never entirely ceased. They included, in addition to the traffic in horses, merchandise, works of art and artists, that in books and maps, that is, scientific information. We know, for example, that the workshops of Venice were in 1559 preparing a mappa mundi in Turkish for Ottoman use.[5] The

Ottomans did not hesitate to copy maps drawn up in Venice or to import volumes of the *Navigationi et Viaggi*. La Serenissima here played the role of intermediary, as prestigious as it was privileged. The Anonymous Chronicler of Istanbul was probably correct in stating that no subject of the Ottoman Empire had as yet visited America; is he to be trusted, however, when he adds that he had no informant locally? His sources in Italian and Spanish suggest the contrary. They must, after all, not only have been imported, but also translated and discussed. Further, someone must have alerted him to their significance. All of which strengthens the hypothesis that our author belonged to a polyglot milieu, keenly interest in cosmography and universal history, but eager, above all, for news of the New World.[6]

Did Turkey already have a historiography or a body of knowledge relating to America on which the Anonymous Chronicler could draw? Thomas D. Goodrich is doubtful, given the non-cumulative nature of this knowledge; the Ottoman authors who were interested in America did not read each other, indeed were even unaware of each other's existence. The *Tarih-i Hind-i garbi* had more luck because it circulated quite widely in manuscript and because it was translated into Persian in the seventeenth century,[7] before being printed in Istanbul at the beginning of the eighteenth century. It was published just as it stood, proof of its originality and prestige in the eyes of the elites of Istanbul, but symptomatic also of a strange lethargy with regard to knowledge. In the Ottoman defence, we should remember that their historical and religious horizons inclined them to look more towards the worlds of Islam and also that, though the Spanish wrote prolifically about the Americas, the number of Europeans who were more interested in Turkey and Asia was far greater. European or Ottoman, it was primarily the East, the Holy Places, the Persia of the Safavids, the fabulous India of the Great Mughal and the Spice Islands that attracted most attention, not forgetting the Cathay of Marco Polo, which became, during the sixteenth century, the China of the Portuguese. Eastern and Asian tropism dominated the planet, even in a New World that was called *Indias occidentales* and that appeared as the western counterpart of the East Indies.

The information that circulated in Europe had neither the same meaning, the same impact or the same fate as in the Ottoman Empire. The presses of Portugal and Spain, Venice and Antwerp, Lyon and Paris did more than merely popularize the discoveries, stimulate curiosity and enrich their owners; they participated in a culture and an economy of the printed book which had no equivalent in the Muslim world. It would be mistaken, however, to draw too sharp a distinction between the Christian world of print and the Muslim world of manuscript. It would be to forget that the Iberian information on America remained for the most part in manuscript until the nineteenth century, including the principal treatises on the indigenous societies, the reports of the administration and the Church and the early chronicles of the religious orders. The circulation of manuscripts continued to provide a preferred route to knowledge in Europe and America as well as in the Muslim world. It remains the case that, whether deposited in the convents of Spain or the libraries of Italy or remaining in America, these writings of the New World were difficult of access to Ottoman historians, unlike the works disseminated by the Italian presses.

Discoveries and Conquests

In spite of these obstacles and differences, the Anonymous Chronicler was convinced of the need and the urgency of making the New World known to his coreligionists by providing them with 'fresh news' (*Hadis-i nev*), the title originally given to his book.

What sort of image of America did he have? The *Tarih-i Hind-i garbi* is full of facts about the Amerindians and the physical geography and fauna and flora of America,[8] but the historical episodes it includes relate exclusively to the discovery and the conquest, whether of the Antilles, Central America, Mexico or Peru. There is little or nothing about the colonial societies that were constructed in the sixteenth century in the American continent. There are many reasons for this. The sources used concerned only the entry of the New World into the Iberian orbit and the events of its conquest; very little of the accounts of the missionaries was circulating in Europe at this period in printed form, even less in Italian translations.[9] In any case, it is hard to imagine a Muslim lingering over the progress of a 'spiritual con-quest' conducted with apparent success by the 'priests of darkness'. For the Anonymous Chronicler, the traces of Christianization in Yucatan were an opportunity to proffer a strange hypothesis that reflected badly on 'the cursed and misguided ones': faced with the advance of the 'lions of the people of Islam', some Christians, he said, had fled the Maghreb and found refuge on the coasts of the Mayan country. On the other hand, he describes on several occa-sions the religious beliefs and practices of the Indians and he was happy to give an account of myths such as that of the 'Four Suns':

> The sages of Mexico related that the end of the world had occurred four times in the afore-mentioned lands: the first time by flood, so that all the animals perished. The second time it rained fires from heaven, and all the animals and possibly stones and trees were burned. The third time strong winds blew and ruined the homes, and most of the people were changed into monkeys and swine.[10]

Nor did the Anonymous Chronicler fail to describe ritual practices such as human sacrifice, the worship of idols and cannibalism. He applauded the outright condemnation of these errors by the Spanish chroniclers, but he attributed them to ignorance of the sharia.[11] The lack of awareness of the colonial transformations in America, which had by 1580 long progressed past the stage of wars of conquest, is less surprising when we remember that, with rare exceptions, Europeans shared the same myopia. Among the latter was Michel de Montaigne, who devoted more attention to the wisdom of the destruction of the indigenous populations than to the construction of a new world. In Istanbul and Bordeaux alike the encounter and the shock to people loomed so large that no space was left for any discussion of the Spanish America of the end of the sixteenth century. A distorted vision we often still share today when we prefer an exotic and distant America to the America that has become one of the hubs of the western world.

The historical account offered by the Anonymous Chronicler hardly impresses by its originality. It is divided into two parts, one devoted to North and Central America,[12] the other to South America. The author copies the European texts so faithfully that the reader is left perplexed by how close he stays to his sources, in the case both of their factual content and of the value judgements with which they were liberally sprinkled. This is probably the most disquieting aspect of the *Tarih-i Hind-i garbi*, the one that reveals the extraordinary closeness, if not interchangeability, of the Spanish and the Turkish in the matter of imperialism and religious proselytization. Would an Ottoman America have resembled a Latin America? Probably not, but the odds are that the Amerindian populations would have paid an equally high price for their subjection to the other giant of the Old World. Not being people of the Book, the Indians would never have been able to claim the semi-tolerance accorded to Jews and Christians in Islamic lands.[13]

Mexican Gazes at Ottoman History

Did Heinrich Martin display any greater originality when he spoke of Turkey? There is no in situ observation, not even a trace of an Ottoman source, to enrich his descriptions. And, unlike his counterpart in Istanbul, Martin was in no way a pioneer if we relocate him within the context of the Iberian and European output. All through the sixteenth century Spain published translations and first hand accounts of the Turks. One after the other, pamphlets calling for a crusade, travellers' tales and more or less well-documented treatises appeared to inform the Iberians and arouse their fervour against Islam. After the victory of Lepanto, a success over the Ottoman fleet off Greece (1571) as spectacular as it was ephemeral, curiosity about the Ottoman world faded. So Heinrich Martin, when he published his *Repertorio de los tiempos* in 1606, made a major contribution to the revival of interest in the Ottoman Empire in the first decades of the seventeenth century. His may even have been one of the first such works of that century in the Hispanic world, since it was not until 1610 that the Castilian translation of the account of Ogier Ghislain de Busbeq, ambassador of Ferdinand of Hapsburg to Suleiman the Magnificent and an informant of the first order, was printed. The other great titles devoted by Spain to the Ottoman world in the seventeenth century were all later.[14]

The *Repertorio* conducts its readers on a journey through the history of the Ottoman Empire, from its foundation to the 1600s. We learn about the origin of the Turks, their first advances into Asia Minor, their conversion to Islam and their battles against the Christians of the Holy Land up to the assumption of power by a captain named Ottoman around 1300 – this was Osman I (1280–1304). Then come his successors – Murâd I, Bâyezîd I, Mehmed I etc. – each with their wars of conquest. This takes us from the siege of Belgrade to the seizure of Constantinople by Mehmed II in 1453. Though he does not omit the reverses, such as the battle of Ankara in 1402, Martin concentrates in his account on the rise to power of a young empire up to the fall of Byzantium, depicted as a day of particular atrocity: 'In the sack of this town the Turks committed the most enormous cruelties that have ever been seen or heard of, either before or since'.[15] This is a denunciation which goes beyond anti-Turkish rhetoric to address those European nations which had never ceased to reproach the Spanish for their 'cruelties' in America.

After this episode, which brought to an end, he says, 1190 years of Christian presence in Byzantium, our cosmographer plays the political pundit and sets about defining the different zones of intervention of Turkish power. He says enough to provide the Mexican reader with a basic but adequate of the geopolitics of the Near East and the eastern Mediterranean at the end of the fifteenth century. As Heinrich Martin comments on the relations of the Porte with each of its neighbours, the contours emerge of a part of the globe with which the Spanish of Mexico were, it appears, as unfamiliar as many Americans today. With the cosmographer as guide, the reader moves from Asia Minor to Egypt, Palestine, Syria, Persia, the Balkans and Hungary. It had to be recognized that the eastern Mediterranean, long ago the centre of the world for Ptolemy of Alexandria, had fallen in its entirety into the hands of Islam. The latter's grip had been total since the loss of the last Christian foothold in 1522, one year after the fall of Mexico City–Tenochtitlan, when the Turks had seized the island of Rhodes from the knights of St John. On these shores, the glories of Antiquity were no more than a distant memory, as shown by the lamentable fate of Greece, incapable of shaking off the domination which oppressed it: 'Today, everybody knows they are the most demoralized people in Europe, plunged into shameful vices, the larger part subject to the Turks and the rest to the Venetians, letting every opportunity pass to shake off the yoke of the Infidel.'[16]

Heinrich Martin was succinct but accurate. He gives many dates, which are often correct. He did not hesitate to dwell on episodes which the literature and theatre of sixteenth-century Europe had already amply exploited, like the humiliating captivity inflicted by Tamerlaine on the sultan Bâyezîd I in 1402:

Tamerlaine carried him with him and he kept him always
in his company imprisoned in an iron cage, devised in such
a way that every time he mounted his horse he put his feet
on his shoulders and when he ate he had him under the
table with the hounds, and the prisoner ate only what he
was thrown from the table.[17]

This saved the historical account from dryness and excited
the morbid curiosity of the reader – the humiliation of the
Turk a spectacle not to be missed![18] It comes as no surprise, then, that the glorious era of Suleiman the Magnificent gets only a very superficial treatment. One might have
expected a comparison between Charles V and the sultan
– they were born in the same year and contemporaries saw
them as rivals, indeed almost as doubles. But Suleiman,
evoked by a few striking facts, is quickly dismissed, and
the reigns of his successors, Selîm II, Murâd III and
Mehmed III, bring the series to an end. This takes the story
to the beginning of the seventeenth century, which was
when Martin completed and published his *Repertorio*.

Heinrich Martin's sources for Turkey were not as diverse
as those used by the Anonymous Chronicler to describe
the New World. One of the rare historians he cites was
born in Rome and became Venetian, Francesco Sansovino
(1521–1583), whose works included a *Historia Universale
dell'Origine, Guerre et Imperio de Turchi*, the first edition
of which appeared in 1560, and the *Annali turcheschi*
(1571).[19] Yet works of history were not lacking in Mexico.
Martin, a publisher and a bookseller, had close connections with the import of books and the book trade. A
cosmographer, he was in possession of a by no means
negligible personal library. He also had access to the col-
lections preserved in the libraries of the Jesuits, with whom
he was in regular contact, and in those of the great religious orders. It is hardly necessary to emphasize that these
sources were all second or even third hand, often published
in Italian – a point in common with the Anonymous
Chronicler – and they seem not to have been based on any

oral testimony. Martin did not have access to any informant who had been to Constantinople, but nor did he seek
one, which is hardly surprising when we realize what
motivated his investigations.

The World Seen from Mexico

Heinrich Martin's curiosity was not confined to the past
or future of the Turks. History plays an important part in
the *Repertorio*. Concluding his text with a glossed chronology of the sixteenth century, Martin even offers a sort
of short universal history with the title *Brief account of
the time during which notable and memorable things happened both in this New Spain and in the kingdom of
Castile and the other parts of the world*. This document
reveals how he viewed the sixteenth century and, what is
more, how he could persuade his readers to view it in their
turn, a bit like the retrospectives with which we are today
bombarded by the press and television. The text is short
and the facts sufficiently succinct to register with busy or
not especially cultured people, precisely those for whom
Martin had published his *Repertorio*. Well-chosen topics
liven the sometimes arid list of dates and events, combining drama and court intrigue rather in the style of 'The
Life and Death of Mary Stuart' or 'The Loves and Fall of
the Rebel Moriscos'. The method is effective; Martin
invented nothing and Spanish readers loved Hispano-
Moorish romances. However, one also senses that he got
pleasure out of retelling these stories in his *History*.

So, what was the early seventeenth-century reader living
at the heart of the New World expected to remember?
Carved up into a series of episodes, European history
dominates this chronology of the world, as one would
expect. It is a predominantly religious history, which concentrates on the effects of the Reformation in Spain, France
and England. Was Heinrich Martin, in attacking heresy,

seeking to give assurances to the Inquisition, to erase any traces of past suspicion – we should remember his probable ties with Lutheranism? Or should we see this simply as intellectual conformism, encouraged by the orthodoxy which prevailed in a New Spain that ardently supported the Counter-Reformation? He deals rapidly with the Protestant question in Spain through the repression launched against Agustín de Cazalla (1510–59) and the exhumation of the corpse of the doctor Constantino Ponce, burnt in effigy in 1560.[20] In recalling the fate of the two most notable figures of the Iberian Reformation, Martin was paying indirect homage to the efficacy of the Spanish Inquisition, which had succeeded in stifling local Protestantism at birth.

England, on the other hand, had made the wrong choice. Martin took time to explain how a kingdom so pious had been able to lapse into heresy. The account is effective, embellished here and there with telling details. Everything had begun well with the exemplary Catholicism of Henry VII. But the love affair between his son Henry VIII and Anne Boleyn, 'who was known to be his own daughter', led to the exile of Catherine of Aragon, aunt of Charles V, and paved the way for heresy. The execution of Anne Boleyn, accused of incest with her brother, the king's remarriage to Jane Seymour, the abortive return of Catholicism under Mary, wife of Philip II, and, finally, the accession to the throne of Elizabeth, 'who was able to make people believe she was Catholic', had sunk England even further into error. 'This, in short, is the story of the origin of the heresy of England.'[21] All that was missing was a tragic episode to make the picture even blacker and to arouse the reader's pity,[22] an unhappy princess hounded by a cruel queen . . . Every century gets the princess it deserves. So we have a grand finale in the two pages – probably taken from the chronicler Herrera – which are devoted to the 'deplorable story' of Mary Queen of Scots, who had been executed in London 'in the year 1587, on the first of March, at ten o'clock in the morning'.

All this information and all these details were far from irrelevant in Mexico, as Protestant Elizabethan England was a source of considerable concern to the inhabitants of New Spain. The ships of the heretics haunted the waters of the Caribbean and Florida, giving rise to repeated alarms in Spanish America. There were some dates that were not forgotten in Mexico, such as 15 September 1568, the day when, suddenly, off Vera Cruz, there had appeared 'the Englishman John Hawkins with ten ships . . . and a few days later there arrived in the same port the viceroy don Martín Enríquez with thirteen vessels of the fleet'. It had been all the Spanish could do to see off this corsair.[23]

After the Protestants, Martin turned to the question of the Muslims of Spain, as if he was anxious to run through all the dangers that threatened the monarchy. The external Islam was matched by an internal Islam, which was even more alarming. Someone so interested in the Turkish empire could hardly be indifferent to the fate of the Moriscos and their revolt in 1568. 'Because it was a memorable event, it seemed to me right to recall here the substance of the affair and the cause of the uprising as clearly and as briefly as possible.'[24] After a short reminder of the Muslim invasion and occupation of the Peninsula, Martin describes the capture of Granada (1492) and the hopes raised by the conversion of the defeated. This led him to describe the policy of assimilation adopted by the Spanish monarchs, and its failure. 'The conversion of the Moors was a sham.' The resentments of the new converts accumulated. They were expressed in a long-planned revolt which erupted in 1568, led by a young Morisco, don Fernando de Valor. The royal armies eventually won the day, 'and so that the Moriscos did not resume their uprising his majesty ordered that not a single one should remain in the kingdom of Granada, and they were resettled in various parts of the kingdoms of Spain'. When Heinrich Martin was writing, the Crown was still waiting for calm on the external front before embarking on radical measures. It was three years after the publication of the *Repertorio* that the expulsion of the Moriscos began.

But how could he linger over the Moriscos and not speak of the other, equally formidable, enemies of the crown? Foremost among these were the rebels in the Low Countries, one of the jewels in the Spanish Crown. Three key dates appear in the chronology: the outbreak of the troubles in Flanders in 1567; the execution of Counts Egmont and Horn 'in the square in Brussels', in July of the following year; and the assassination of the Prince of Orange, leader of the insurgents, in 1584. When the *Repertorio* was published the truce with Holland had not yet been signed and the rebels were threatening Spanish interests from the Caribbean to Japan.

There remained Mediterranean Islam. The principal episodes in the battle against the Barbary states and the Turks were recalled in quick succession, delineating the other great frontier of Catholic Christendom.[25] They marked a century of advances and retreats: victories like Lepanto, resounding defeats like that of the king of Portugal 'in the plains of Tamita'.[26] Eastern Europe, by contrast, was dealt with only briefly, as if our author was indifferent to the threat which hung over Vienna, so far from the New World and so close to the Ottoman Empire. He attached scarcely any more importance to the bloody wars being fought between Turkey and Persia, observing not without satisfaction that 'the prince of Persia has killed eighty thousand Turks in various confrontations'.[27]

The History of America and of Mexico

This troubled Europe, exposed to the assaults of Muslims and heretics, contrasted with a pacified and stable West Indies. In America, order prevailed. The failure of the civil wars in Peru and the triumph of the Spanish Crown, the uninterrupted succession of viceroys in Lima and Mexico

City and the reassuring presence of the Inquisition in the capital of New Spain systematically reflected the image of a New World spared the turmoil that was disrupting Europe, the Mediterranean and the Iberian Peninsula.

The America of Heinrich Martin was also an expanding world. The Spanish crossed and explored the Pacific and, in the very year in which the Moriscos rebelled (1568), an expedition commanded by Alvaro de Mendaña, heading for New Guinea, discovered the Solomon Islands, to which were given the evocative name of the prestigious king of Israel.[28] Setting out from Peru, ten years later, on another memorable voyage, Pedro Sarmiento de Gamboa passed through the Strait of Magellan and entered the South Atlantic. Difficulties in Europe, faraway feats – the contrast between the Indies and the Peninsula could hardly be sharper. Colonial America was given its rightful place in the concert of Christian kingdoms and not squeezed out by the obsession with the noble savage or the obligatory denunciation of the cruelties of the Conquest.

Yet this continental and maritime vision was very far from ignoring the pre-Hispanic past. Here Heinrich Martin was probably not a pioneer, except in that the pages he devoted to the subject were among the first of their type to have been published by the presses of the New World. Nor was his information at all original. For his description of the foundation of Mexico City and the succession of Aztec sovereigns, he was spoiled for choice, although he revealed a strong preference for the *Natural and Moral History* of José de Acosta, which he pillaged like all the compilers of his day. Published in 1590, this history of the Indies had enjoyed considerable success and been translated into every European language. Martin could hardly have made a better choice. But not everything in the *Repertorio* was second hand. Martin was also interested in the Indian sources, in particular in the calendar of the ancient Mexicans. There was no doubt in his eyes that they had been capable of writing the history of their country: 'Before the arrival of the Spanish', he explains:

> they lived in a civilized way and used systems to count and to measure, and also characters with which they indicated the epochs and represented the things that befell them . . . in a manner so ordered and so concerted that these characters served them as *histories* since, thanks to them, they knew what had happened in past centuries.[29]

Martin could not have been ignorant of the fact that, at the time of writing, in Mexico City and its valley, indigenous and mestizo scholars were making great efforts to collect colonial or pre-Hispanic pictographic sources and interpret and transcribe them using the Latin alphabet. Cristóbal del Castillo, Fernando de Alva Ixtlilxóchitl, Domingo Chimalpahin were among those, Indian and mestizo, who participated in this project to preserve indigenous memories. At a time when the Indian populations were disappearing, decimated by epidemics, this rescue operation made the city of Mexico and its region a locus for historical thinking and production which was exceptional in the western world.

The History of the World Seen from Istanbul

The Anonymous Chronicler had no such desire to offer his contemporaries a lesson in sixteenth-century history. Most of his historical information concerned the conquest of the New World. It is abundant and it is all taken from the Spanish and Italian sources mentioned above. Nevertheless, there are also in his text a wealth of historical references which reveal horizons as surprisingly open as those of Heinrich Martin, with certain strong points. Thus when he discusses in detail the background to the initiatives and departure of Christopher Columbus, he cannot stop himself from commenting on the fall of Granada. The importance he attaches to the past and to the annihilation of Muslim Spain, to which he several times returns, may even indicate that he himself had Iberian origins, or at least close links with some Muslims driven out of the Peninsula.

The Mediterranean is also central to a series of episodes such as the conquest of Andalusia by Târiq, the resistance of the Maghreb to Spanish penetration, the exploits of Khayredîn Pasha (Barbarossa) and the exemplary influence of Muslim Sicily for the faithful of Islam, as well as the attempts to cut through the Isthmus of Suez. Rather than Islamocentrism, we should perhaps speak of a sort of Mediterranean ethnocentrism. If we add to this the denunciation of the advance of the Portuguese in the Indian Ocean and the Spanish in the New World, it emerges that the majority of the Anonymous Chronicler's historical references relate to confrontations with the Christians; it is as if the world of Islam could hardly imagine itself without Christendom once it chose to adopt a global and planetary perspective that included the New World. This Islam, which did not accept the loss of its positions in the western Mediterranean, could not but be sensitive to the danger the Christian conquest of America represented for the 'the foundation of religion and the world'.[30]

A Mexican Gaze in Mexico City, an Iberian Gaze in Istanbul?

Heinrich Martin had geographical reasons for paying particular attention to the place in which he lived, worked and wrote, namely the singularity of the locales, the climate, the atmosphere and the sky. He had authorial and editorial reasons, too. Since the works imported from Europe satisfied neither the needs nor the tastes of the inhabitants of New Spain, their content had to be adapted to local realities so as not to frighten away readers. What suits Europe does not necessarily suit the rest of the world. One can imagine that his fifteen years in Mexico, after some thirty years in Europe, had given Martin more than just a sharper sense of the diversity of climates, tastes and ways of life. He was convinced that European knowledge would export all the more easily if it could be made into a western knowledge, relevant to other parts of the world. His threefold experience as European, author and publisher all helped Martin to learn the lessons of a global approach to America and the world; although he never forgot the necessity – then as now – of 'pleasing the reader'.

Heinrich Martin the historian thus made the same shift as Heinrich Martin the geographer and publisher, that is, to Mexico. The Mexican past, that history before the Spanish, provided additional colour and anchorage. It is surely because he lived in Mexico City, and because this city had a very long history, that he dated his lunar calendar (*lunario*) not only from the year 1606 since the birth of Christ and the year 5558 since the Creation of the world, but also from the years 483 since the foundation of Mexico City, 114 since the Discovery of the New World and 86 since the conquest of Mexico.[31] 'Mexicanization' did not mean retreating into or turning in on oneself. The New Spain described by Heinrich Martin looked first and foremost towards western Europe and South America, but it was also interested in the Pacific, Asia and the Ottoman East. Only Africa is missing, and this in spite of the many black slaves who lived in Mexico, whereas the presence of China can be sensed lurking in the shadow of the Philippines. Martin made no claim to be comprehensive. Far from engaging in an exercise in universal or imperial history, he was simply trying to understand the pre-Hispanic and colonial past of his adopted country from a global perspective. By the same token, the Eurocentrism which invariably handicapped the European histories is muted, though without the *Repertorio* being for a moment anything other than a text conceived and compiled by a European. Set against the official chroniclers of Madrid and their swaggering Hispanocentrism, Martin reminds us that the Catholic monarchy did not speak with a single voice.[32]

It was not by chance, therefore, that, a few years later, an attentive reader of Martin, the indigenous chronicler

Chimalpahin, drew on the *Repertorio* for material that would enable him to put the history of his ancestors in an Atlantic and planetary context. Nor was it coincidence that this educated Indian was careful to record in his *Journal* the major events of the wider world, a world which included Paris, Rome and Japan. Both Heinrich Martin and Chimalpahin kept one eye glued on the wider world, though without conforming to the European standards that were being developed at that time.

The Anonymous Chronicler of Istanbul, in contrast, had difficulty finding his way. It was hard for him to maintain his Islamic and Mediterranean vision in the face of the Hispanocentrism of his sources for the New World. It is the gaze at America of the Spanish and Italian chroniclers that his text projects, from start to finish, even if he now and again interjects calls to Islamic order, though not often enough to reorient or invert the point of view. The Turkish narrative reproduces the voice of the conquistadors with remarkable, not to say wearisome, fidelity; to the point where one is driven to ask whether this imitation and this intellectual dependence might have other causes than the novelty of the subject. Are they perhaps due to the absence of a gaze formed in observation of the western world in its entirety? Had Istanbul, by turning its back on the Christian world, ended up lacking the tools for a more critical or more inventive observation? The task was certainly easier for the German, who had the benefit of the substantial European output already devoted to Turkey. Too little experience on the shores of the Bosphorus, too much information in New Spain.

But the more or less freely admitted biases of our two authors do not explain the tension visible within each of these texts. Why, in Mexico, put so much emphasis on describing a Turkey so remote from America? What was it in Istanbul that drove the Anonymous Chronicler to devote so many pages to the New World? Curiosity about the things of the world and the 'desire to know' – what time is it there? – cannot alone explain this phenomenon.

– 6 –

The History of the World is Written in the Stars

Many astrologers, and in particular the Arabs, believe that the destruction of monarchies, the transformations of empires, wars, epidemics, earthquakes, floods and other events of this type, apart from the will of God, are due to the conjunctions and the encounter of the planets.
Heinrich Martin, *Repertorio de los tiempos*, p. 237

It is requested of His Glorious Majestic Excellency that in the future the bloodthirsty sword of the people of Islam reach that advantageous land [the New World] and that its regions and districts be filled with the lights of the religious ceremonies of Islam and that the possessions and goods that have been mentioned and the other treasures of the unbelievers marked by disgrace be divided, with the permission of the Lord God, among the masters of the Holy War and the nation full of driving force.[1]

It is with this major project that the Anonymous Chronicler of Istanbul ends his account of the conquest of Mexico, directly addressing the sultan Murâd III. More than twenty years later, in Mexico City, Heinrich Martin made an equally belligerent appeal, but in the opposite direction: 'May our Lord in his infinite goodness and mercy deign to rid us of this horrible and destructive Beast!'[2] One recognizes in the Beast the monster of the Apocalypse (13:1), which St John saw coming up out of the sea:

> having ten horns and seven heads, and on his horns ten diadems, and upon his heads names of blasphemy. And the beast which I saw was like unto a leopard, and his feet were as the feet of a bear, and his mouth as the mouth of a lion: and the dragon gave him his power, and his throne, and great authority. And I saw one of his heads as though it had been smitten unto death; and his death-stroke was healed: and the whole earth wondered after the beast; and they worshipped the dragon, because he gave his authority unto the beast; and they worshipped the beast, saying, Who is like unto the beast? and who is able to war with him?

War against the Infidel

The enthusiasm with which the Anonymous Chronicler gathered his information was in the spirit of a resurgent Islam. Sicily, that 'unique thing of the time and the rarity of the era', lost since the eleventh century and Spanish in 1580, had already been the subject of a pathetic exhortation: 'may the force of the strength of the Ottoman Empire increase daily, so that with the least effort it may cleanse the holy places that exist on the afore-mentioned island of the filths of ignorance and unbelief'.[3] For our Ottoman, there could be no question of abandoning the new territories across the ocean to the Infidel. Every effort must be made to organize their conquest. The 'news' he collected was intended to convince the sultan to direct his armies towards this part of the world. This 'India' invaded and converted by the Christians must be retaken, cleansed and converted by the soldiers of Islam. But the vehement appeal that rings out in his text went unanswered. The Ottoman sultan was in this regard as cautious as his rival Philip II. And in practice the Ottoman advance towards the Atlantic came up against the kingdom of Morocco, whose resistance barred the way to the great Ocean. Without direct sea access, any American project remained a chimera.

The cry of the Anonymous Chronicler irresistibly recalls the appeals for the conquest of China resounding at the same time within the Catholic monarchy, where some Spaniards were envisaging an attack on the Celestial Empire from the Philippines. The same lack of moderation is visible on both sides. From now on, however, the dynamics of planetary expansion and domination favoured the Christian camp at the expense of that of Islam. Yet there was, in the end, no Spanish conquest of China, nor any Turkish conquest of America. It remains the case that these yearnings on both sides reveal how relations between Christendom and Islam had by this date acquired an intercontinental and even planetary context. They were a manifestation of a world consciousness which was not confined to Europeans. For, over and above its military and religious significance, the appeal of the Anonymous Chronicler seems also to express a fundamental question which was inseparable from this mind-set: how to accept and think the 'post-Columbian' world, now that it had acquired another continent and that it could be circumnavigated? How to attach the New World to the Old, and correct the major 'blip' exploited by the Christians, if not by making America Islamic? This was a price that had to be paid if the gulf between it and the Dâr al-islâm was to be made good.

From Astronomy to Astrology

Heinrich Martin was less belligerent. Comfortably established in his printing house in Mexico City, surrounded by his books, his maps and his measuring devices, Martin looked to the sky for what his counterpart in Istanbul looked to from Holy War. His vision of the history of the world was primarily a product of his astronomical and astrological preoccupations. He was not a professional historian and, if he took a close interest in Ottoman history, it was because he was anxious to verify the accuracy of the predictions for the fate of this empire.[4] In his eyes, the succession of the Ottoman rulers established irrefutably that this empire was coming to an end: Ahmed I, son of Mehmed III, would be the last sultan.

The genre chosen by Heinrich Martin lent itself easily to considerations of this sort.[5] Plentifully represented in Spain, it dealt with astronomy, astrology, cosmography and meteorology, with the aim of responding to the questions of readers put off by excessive erudition and rhetorical virtuosity. Andrés de Li at Zaragoza in 1495, Bernardo Pérez de Vargas in 1563, Rodrigo Zamorano in 1585, Jerónimo de Chávez, Martin and Jerónimo Cortés and Juan Alemán had all published 'repertories' which were popular in America.[6] The European repertories passing for the best in the world, it is hardly surprising that the Jesuit Matteo Ricci should take it upon himself to correct those of the Chinese.[7] This literature was also of interest to the Indians of Mexico, who were inspired by it to compile calendars liberally sprinkled with European borrowings.[8] The investigations conducted by missionaries such as Bernardino de Sahagún into the astronomical knowledge of the ancient Mexicans had led educated Indians and Europeans to compare the learning of each in this sphere. Correspondences seemed to exist between the two conceptions of the world. Like Aristotle, the indigenous scholars imagined a number of skies piled up above the surface of the earth. Most of all, however, Europeans and Indians shared the same curiosity about what the future held. They were all, for example, interested in eclipses, which they believed exerted a baleful influence on earthly life.

By publishing his *Repertorio* in Mexico, Heinrich Martin took his place within a local tradition. Some twenty years earlier, in 1587, Diego García de Palacio had published an *Instrucción nauthica* which dealt with the great principles of astronomy. It also offered a 'rustic astrology' based on knowledge of the stars and their influences. Written in the form of dialogues, the *Instrucción* was aimed at sailors and others interested in maritime matters.[9] It was a popularizing work, as, in its turn, was the *Repertorio* of Heinrich Martin. Popularization is often felt as a constraint by scholars, but it was the ignorance and rapacity of the Spanish of Mexico which more concerned our author in 1606. The New World was not Europe. In his Prologue, with scant concern to offer an introduction appealing to his readers, Martin gave vent to the low esteem in which he held Mexican society.

His *Repertorio* adhered to the rules of the genre. After a presentation of the cosmos, it explained the sky and the stars, defined time and its divisions, analysed the signs of the zodiac and surveyed the planets, before offering a lunar calendar and meteorological predictions for the years 1606–20.[10] This was followed by astrology, explicitly the subject of the fourth part. In fact astrological science dominates the book from beginning to end. It explains its heterogeneous, not to say disjointed, form. Astrology, claims Heinrich Martin, was a science indispensable to agriculture as also to the prevention, diagnosis and treatment of illnesses.[11] But his curiosity also extended to the celestial phenomena whose consequences might have incalculable political importance, like, for example, 'the conjunction of the planets Jupiter and Saturn', which happened on 24 December 1603, in the 'ninth degree of the sign of Sagittarius'.

It was in this context that Heinrich Martin explored the history of the Ottomans. The astronomer observed, the astrologer interpreted. Why, then, were the conjunctions of the planets of so much concern? They exercised a decisive influence on the fate of kingdoms: 'Many astrologers, and in particular the Arabs, believe that the destruction of monarchies, the transformations of empires, wars, epidemics, earthquakes, floods and other events of this type' are due to the conjunctions of the planets. This was the case, most notably, with the 'very great conjunctions which happen every eight hundred years in the sign of the Ram'. But 'great conjunctions', too, were to be feared. They were more frequent and took place 'in signs of analogous nature every one hundred and ninety six years'.[12] Great or very great conjunctions – we have come a long way from medicine and meteorological predictions!

Fateful Dates[13]

The interest shown by our German in the Turks comes oddly at a time when Spain appeared to be disengaging from the Mediterranean in order to concentrate on the defence of the Atlantic. According to Fernand Braudel, the years 1578–83 marked a turning point, a *fin de siècle*. The views of the great historian may today need qualification, but that Philip II was from this time seeking peace rather than war with the Ottomans is not in doubt.[14] The silence of Spanish literature with regard to the Turks may be explained by the victory of Lepanto and the difficulties being experienced by the Ottoman Empire, which produced a temporary lull in Spanish interest in the Ottoman world,[15] or by the fact that the Barbary states had supplanted the Sublime Porte in Iberian preoccupations. What, then, are we to make of the initiative of Heinrich Martin and the curiosity of his Mexican readers? If there was one issue preoccupying the Spanish authorities in 1606 it was the expulsion of the Moriscos. This was achieved between 1609 and 1614, finally bringing to an end nine hundred years of Muslim presence on the soil of the Peninsula.

Yet Heinrich Martin was not alone in thinking about the end of the Ottomans. In 1605, a year before the appearance of the *Repertorio*, an ambassador of the French king, Henri IV, to the Sublime Porte, François Savary de Brèves, published a *Short discourse on the sure means for the destruction and ruination of the Ottoman princes*. Was Paris fighting the same battles as Mexico City? Not really; our cosmographer dealt with the question in his own way, that is, from a great distance and through astrology. Not content with sharing the hostility of many of his contemporaries towards the Muslim world in all its forms – Turks, Barbary coasters, Moriscos – Heinrich Martin claimed to predict when the rival of the Catholic monarchy would disappear and to be breaking this news to his readers in New Spain. He was careful to surround himself with numerous precautions in the face of a Church increasingly distrustful of astrology. His proof was made in total orthodoxy and under cover of the tribunal of the Holy Office of the Inquisition, of which Martin did not forgot he was a 'familiar'. Why did an institution usually so punctilious not seek to prohibit publication of the *Repertorio*? The cosmographer-printer's acceptance into the elites of the capital of New Spain must have won out over the suspicions that might have been aroused by the wild ideas of a German acquainted with Lutheranism or the doings of a mage over-anxious to be of service.[16]

So, when was the Turkish empire at last to collapse? The answer lay in the stars and the prophecies. First among the latter were those of the sibyl Erythrea, who had predicted the crushing of the Turks and the Muslim communities.[17] It was not by chance that Heinrich Martin began with the almost canonical list of the prophecies of the sibyls. Supposed to have predicted the coming of Christianity, these priestesses of Antiquity had sparked, over time, an abundant literature which tickled the curiosity of the scholars of the Renaissance. The artists of the period liked to celebrate them and their haughty silhouettes were even depicted on the walls of the convents and palaces of New Spain, as we are reminded by the beautiful Amazons of the Casa del Dean in Puebla.[18]

Archaeological finds added their quota of proof. The patriarch of Constantinople Gennadios II (Georgios Scholarios, 1400–73) was said to have read the prediction of the fall of the Ottomans 'inscribed and depicted' on an ancient column in the imperial capital.[19] Some German sources, in particular the mysterious documents excavated at Magdeburg in 1430, had foretold the coming of a prince called Charles, who would reign over the whole of Europe and bring assistance to a Church in turmoil. After 'terrible disruptions of kingdoms', the Eagle and the Lion would become masters of the world and Christians would at last be able to circulate safely throughout Asia. 'This forecast', explained Heinrich Martin, 'alludes to the advent of the sects of Calvin, Luther, Zwingli and many others . . . as for the fact that Christians will be able to circulate freely in Asia, this predicts the fall of the Turkish empire and the transformation of the Mahometan sect; the Eagle and the Lion signify the emperor and the king of Spain.' Nostradamus, as a loyal courtier of the king of France, applied the prophecy of Magdeburg to Charles IX . . .

The European learning of Heinrich Martin could not but impress his Mexican readers and win them over to his astrological science; especially as his facts were largely unverifiable. Thus a mass of signs, predictions and fateful events added further support to the cosmographer's proof. It becomes clear that historical accounts interested Martin only for the astrological material they contained. He may have consulted the *Theatrum* of Abraham Ortelius,[20] and he may have made use of the Italian Francesco Sansovino, who had studied 'the universal history of the Turks', but it was in the astrologers that he was primarily interested, a circle of internationally renowned experts that included Gerónimo Lafantino, Lucas Gauricus, Nostradamus, Antonio Torqato of Ferrara and even Vicente Baldino. They had all forecast major events, which had for the most part been proved true, and they were all agreed in predicting 'the fall and destruction of the Turkish Empire'.[21] It is to the excellent physician and astrologer of Ferrara, Antonio Torqato, that we owe a famous prediction, *De eversione Europae prognosticon*, which the cosmographer of Mexico inevitably cited. Widely known since the end of the fifteenth century, and printed and constantly reprinted since, the *De eversione* had become a classic of the genre. In addition to several major episodes of European history, among them the imprisonment of Francis I and the union of Portugal and Castile, Torqato had provided precise details concerning the life expectancy of the Ottoman Empire. It was not enough to predict the imminence of its fall, which for many people went without saying, what really mattered was to determine the precise moment.[22]

Nothing could be simpler, according to the mage of Ferrara or Heinrich Martin: the accession of the fourteenth or fifteenth Turkish emperor would sound its death knell.[23] The last sultan would without any doubt be the worst enemy of Christendom. He would ravage the Christian world 'by sea and by land',[24] and even attack the coasts of Spain. The blow suffered would be terrible. But Christians would overcome their differences and, united against the Turks, would vanquish the sultan, who would lose his life. Cashing in on the political crisis triggered by his death, the Christians would then need only to subject the East to our Holy Mother Church. It remained to identify this last emperor whose reign would be so disastrous for the Ottoman Empire. Was it Ahmed I, who had begun to rule in 1603? In which case the publication of the *Repertorio de los tiempos* in Mexico City in 1606 was highly topical. It was for the reader to decide. In any case, the history of the world which fascinated Heinrich Martin was essentially that of the immediate present.

The fact is, Heinrich Martin was interested only in those historical events which had been foretold by astrologers. Indeed, one gets the feeling that, to his mind, a fact was made all the more striking and all the more significant by having been predicted; this was what made it an event. Such was the case in 1571 with the seizure of Cyprus by the Turks and the battle of Lepanto, the Turkish entry to La Goulette in 1574, the revolt in Flanders, the outbreak of the Turco-Persian war in 1577 and even, the year after, the 'disastrous loss of the king of Portugal in Africa', in other words, his defeat at Kasr al-Kabîr. Given that all these events had been predicted and that they had duly come about, the reader would infer that other predictions would unfailingly one day be realized. And what could be less open to dispute in this regard than the prophecies of those concerned, that is, 'what the Turks themselves say and what they have from their ancestors'?[25] Martin was here referring to Muslim millenarianism. Mahomet was said to have predicted that his law would last for a thousand years. All it needed was an elementary calculation: if you took as point of departure the birth of the prophet (which Martin put in 592), the fateful day had passed, but if you accepted that of the preaching of the Koran (632, said Martin), the Muslims' year one thousand was well within sight and one could justifiably continue to hope. To crown it all, and to return to the stars, a huge comet had appeared in the Mexican sky at the beginning of October 1604, when the *Repertorio* was being written, and its passage had lasted more than a year. Comets, the readers of Heinrich Martin were well aware, always presaged calamities.

Comets, Mahometan traditions, German, French and Italian predictions, ancient prophecies reinterpreted in the Middle Ages – like most of his contemporaries, Heinrich Martin used any means to hand to predict when the end of the Turks would come. But it was probably the dream of 'Amurat' – Murâd III (1547–95) – which fascinated him most. Sick and bedridden, the son of Selîm II had seen in a dream a gigantic figure which had one foot placed on the tower of the Great Mosque of Constantinople and the other on the 'cape of the sea'. Arms raised towards the sky, he held the sun in one hand and the moon in the other. With the foot placed on the minaret, the giant destroyed the mosque and the palace of Murâd. Horrified, the sultan woke with a start and summoned his mages, who made haste to comfort him with assurances that the prodigy presaged a catastrophe for Christendom.[26] With his habitual aplomb, Heinrich Martin made short work of the Turkish interpretation. The gigantic figure, by his telling, was no other than God, who held in his hands both the Christians (the sun) and the Muslims (the moon). It was obvious that the destruction of the mosque and palace prefigured that of the 'cursed sect' and the 'monarchy of the Turkish Empire'. And what better to confirm this dire warning than the death of the sultan, five days later. Murâd was succeeded by Mehmed III (1595–1603), the third of his name and the fourteenth emperor according to Heinrich Martin. The countdown had surely begun.[27]

An Astronomical and Astrological Vision of the World

So the disproportionate attention our German paid to the Ottoman Empire was a direct product of his astrological preoccupations. He discussed the Turkish case in the section of the *Repertorio* in which he examined 'the great conjunction of the planets Jupiter and Saturn which happened on 24 December 1603, in the ninth degree of the sign of Sagittarius'. But this is just one example among many. In expatiating on the subject of the Ottoman Empire, as in interspersing his treatise with historical and geographical digressions, Heinrich Martin was aiming to kill two birds with one stone. By concrete examples that were more or less familiar to his readers he demonstrated the value of astronomy and astrology, while at the same time expounding his own way of seeing the world and its history. In his mind, as in that of the majority of his contemporaries, astronomy and astrology were inseparable. A major catastrophe like the decimation of the Indian populations of Mexico was immediately interpreted in the light of these disciplines. Placed under the ascendancy of Capricorn, it seemed natural that Mexico, specifically its autochthonous populations, should be exposed to catastrophes every time this sign was affected by comets or harmful conjunctions of planets: Spanish conquest, smallpox epidemic of 1520 ('history relates that it was impossible to bury all those who died even though this sickness, in spite of its cruelty, spared the Spanish'),[28] epidemic of

1546 and epidemic of 1576, which claimed more than two million victims.

Prodigious signs generally accompanied the great events and the great 'changes' – or *mudanzas* – to which they led. The Bible was full of them – Exodus, Kings, Isaiah, Maccabees, St Luke, The Acts of the Apostles, the Apocalypse . . . They were numerous in the historians of Antiquity: Flavius Josephus and Eusebius of Caesarea 'related great and numerous prodigies which preceded the destruction of Jerusalem and the last captivity of its wretched inhabitants'.[29] The history of change is history as catastrophe. Heinrich Martin provides an accelerated history of the great invasions and the annihilated empires, beginning with the barbarian invasions which had ravaged the Roman Empire: in 572 the Lombards descended on Italy, in 912 it was the turn of the Hungarians, in 712 the Saracens swooped down on the Iberian Peninsula, in 1180 the 'Moors' took Jerusalem and 'stole' the Holy Land,[30] in 1453 the Turks seized Constantinople, then it was the turn of Egypt and Hungary . . . The whole was spiced up with atrocities of every type, rapes, profanations, infanticides, barbarous cruelties, tyrannies and monstrosities, not counting a collection of prodigies each more terrible than the last.

A historical upheaval never happened alone, as demonstrated by a series of examples not only from Europe but from Africa and Asia, too. Before the revolt of the Moriscos and the outbreak of the last war of Granada, in 1568, many people had seen, in a clear, serene sky, 'a sort of band which stretched from Alpujarra to the West and on it appeared . . . rocks, trees and mountains, and people bearing arms and people in mourning, and there were also at this period births of monstrous animals'. A little later, the Moriscos had rebelled, leaving tens of thousands dead in the Andalusian mountains. And what was true of Granada was also true of Portugal. The shield and sword of the king of Portugal Afonso Enriques (1109–85), placed in the monastery of Santa Cruz of Coïmbra, had twice fallen from the wall where they hung. The first time it was to foretell the death of King John III, the second, in 1576, came at the very moment that King Sebastian took the disastrous decision to go to Africa and attack the forces of Moley Mahomed in the 'kingdoms of Morocco and Fez'. Two years later, the Portuguese sovereign had perished at the battle of Kasr al-Kebîr, 'meeting his death in Africa along with the flower of his kingdom'.[31] Two years later, for lack of a direct heir, his crown had fallen into the hands of his cousin Philip II. And, in case the prodigies of Coïmbra had not been enough to sound the alarm, a great comet, which appeared in November 1577 in the sign of Libra, had confirmed the imminent end of Sebastian and the unhappy fate which awaited the kingdom of Portugal. From Portugal to Africa and from Africa to Spain, the omens related continents and shaped the history of the world.

The astrologer of Mexico thought nothing of referring to events taking place at more or less the same time but on the other side of the world, and his interest in Japan was far from random. Ever since the Jesuit Francis Xavier had set foot in the archipelago, Japan had attracted numerous Iberian missionaries and merchants. The establishment of the Spanish in the Philippines had brought Asia closer to Mexico, and made Japan a focal point for royal officials, merchants and monks, all of whom saw it as a providential springboard for the fabulous land of China. The event that caught the attention of Heinrich Martin was the death, in 1582, of a great Japanese lord, Oda Nobunaga.[32] This *daimyo* had seized a large part of the country; the deadly efficacy of firearms had brought him victory at the battle of Nagashino (1575). Seven years later, on his way to put down a revolt, he had paused in a temple at Kyoto, the Honnô-ji, where one of his lieutenants made a surprise attack on him. Nobunaga allegedly then took his own life, unless he had been killed in the confrontation. His death opened the gates of power to one of his generals, Hideyoshi, and hastened the unification of Japan.

The death of Nobunaga had been foretold by a string of prodigies: a reddening sky, a great nocturnal brightness, an unparalleled comet, an enormous ball of fire. According to Heinrich Martin, who resembled his European sources in having difficulty in grasping the Japanese political system, the 'emperor' had built a sumptuous temple in which an effigy commemorating the day of his birth was worshipped. A pride so immoderate and so idolatrous could not go unpunished, even in a pagan country; nor could the punishment go unseen. As in any other part of the world, prodigies predicted the imminence of the punishment reserved by heaven for the impious sovereign. In Japan, it seems, heaven has a long memory, since the centuries have done little to improve this sad reputation. Now a character in manga and video games, Oda Nobunaga has remained the wicked man endowed with a power with monstrous origins who made such an impression on Heinrich Martin and European observers.

Not long after, the archipelago was the scene of the first truly 'international' event in its history, in the eyes of a Christian from Europe, that is, the martyrdom of the Franciscans of Nagasaki in 1597. This tragedy, too, had been preceded by heavenly signs: 'The year before, 1596, in the month of July, just as the galleon called the San Felipe was leaving Capul [in the Philippines], its passengers saw a huge comet; then, on 18 September, there appeared in front of the ship a horrifying whale. They took all this as presaging the evil that awaited them; because after suffering a terrible shipwreck, they reached Japan, where the ship and the silver was confiscated and they risked losing their lives, victims of numerous misadventures at the hands of these barbarians.' Some Franciscans who had been on this voyage were tortured and executed by crucifixion after their arrest in Nagasaki.

A sudden shift to the Iberian Peninsula, and an event rather closer to home, served to remind the reader that ominous signs were a fact of life in Spain, too, and that this country was safe neither from catastrophes nor divine punishments. An Aragonese bell tower, which was accustomed to ring of its own accord to foretell calamities, had tolled in 1601 in the valley of the Ebro, not long before epidemics had broken out throughout the country.

The Aztecs were Right

Why look so far afield? Heinrich Martin need only have directed his gaze at Mexico and the prodigies which had preceded the fall of Moctezuma's empire, about which he was well informed. Monsters with two heads, celestial phenomena, inexplicable events and disturbing appearances and disappearances had punctuated the last years of the master of Mexico, although his soothsayers had been unable to interpret them satisfactorily. The last prodigy had been by no means the least threatening. A farmer had been working in his field when he had been carried off by a huge eagle, which had set him down deep in a cave. A mysterious voice had then asked if he recognized the person lying stretched out on the ground. The farmer identified Moctezuma from his royal accoutrements. The voice announced that the sovereign would soon pay for his crimes and his recklessness, then instructed the peasant to burn the prince on his thigh. Initially reluctant, the peasant eventually did as he was told. He was then ordered to seek out Moctezuma in his palace and tell him everything that had happened. The eagle having returned him to the place from which he had first seized him, the farmer made his way to the sovereign, who then looked at his thigh, saw that he had been burned and 'was extremely sad and troubled'.[33]

There is more than a trace here of José de Acosta's *Natural and Moral History of the Indies*.[34] Heinrich Martin was simply repeating tales of prodigies already endlessly told and retold and circulating all over Mexico, both Indian and Spanish. If they appealed to Martin, it was not so much because they demonstrated the ineluctable nature of the Mexican defeat as because they testified to the infallibility of the indigenous predictions, hence to the universal validity of astrology. He even allowed himself the luxury of introducing into his Mexican account an episode taken from a history of Charles V.[35] It concerned prodigies that had occurred in the region of Bergamo, thousands of miles from the New World, in 1517. At that time, when Europe was as yet ignorant of the existence of Mexico, the Bergamo region had been the scene of fantastic nocturnal battles on an apocalyptic scale, which indubitably presaged tragic events. The prodigy was soon known in large parts of Europe and it quickly became the subject of numerous interpretations which combined eschatological concerns and fear of the Turks.[36] The chronicler who inspired Heinrich Martin had clearly not been thinking of Mexico, and the history of Europe had provided him with plenty of choice. The astrologer of Mexico City, faced with these sensational events, did not hesitate to place before his readers this obvious fact: the prodigies of Bergamo might just as well have foretold the conquest of Mexico: 'The devil who was their inventor predicted them because of our sins and showed them while rejoicing in the benefit he hoped to gain from them.'[37]

In fact at this same period, on the lake of Mexico, some fishermen had captured a bird which looked like, but was not, a crane; the creature was taken to Moctezuma who observed that the strange fowl had on its head a sort of mirror. This mirror showed the sky and the stars although they had all gone from the Mexican firmament. Then the Indians saw in the mirror 'warriors . . . coming from the east . . . armed, fighting and killing'. Could it be that the apparitions of the Bergamo region had also occurred in Mexico? The oracles of Moctezuma were unable to explain the prodigy and the bird suddenly disappeared. We may note that the local soothsayers, Turkish or Mexican, were never as perceptive as Heinrich Martin, as if, even in the sphere of astrology, the Christian world always had to be one step ahead.

The priority given to the theme of the fall of empires and premonitory signs explains why Heinrich Martin, in his historical vision, chose to deal with the predicted end of the Mexicans (1521) before even starting on the discovery of the New World (1492), in defiance of chronology. The inversion is significant. It expresses once again a local standpoint which broke with the ethnocentrism of the European chroniclers and historians. It was no accident that Martin adopted a Mexican perspective when he spoke of 'the coming of Hernán Cortés [into this country]'.[38] The two histories, that of Europe and that of Mexico, had long consisted of parallel and independent series of events, until the celestial language of signs and prodigies related them to each other. In demonstrating this link between the two worlds, our German made manifest a causality which transcended continents and preceded the fusion of the two histories under the influence of the Spanish conquest. The signs predicting the Spanish invasion had been inscribed on Mexico's tropical sky, just as Europe resounded with prodigies foretelling the fate of the Mexican Empire. Bringing the astrological facts together in this way anticipated and in effect legitimated the annexation of Mexico by Spain.

Global History and the End of the World

Heinrich Martin may have had a taste for history and historians – he was an ardent reader of the 'chronicles and histories of reliable authors' – but he was first and foremost an astrologer who wanted to understand world events and who believed he could decipher them with the help of the stars. He needed the history of the world, therefore, to demonstrate the value of his system; the diversity of periods, societies, situations and events simply confirmed his interpretations. In their turn, however, these same interpretations led him back to a global history, as if the old astrological code – to be handled diplomatically so as not to disturb the Inquisition and so as to safeguard the idea of free will – made it possible to think the world with the confidence of a science and the precision of mathematics.

Astrology also explains his interest in other societies. Heinrich Martin had the flair and the aplomb to add to the European sources of the fifteenth and sixteenth centuries the chronicles and annals of the Indians of Mexico. These sources predating the arrival of the Spanish showed that Indian history could be explained exactly like European and Asian history, because in this case, too, prodigious signs preceded catastrophic events. This similarity was proof that the Mexican sources ought not to be considered fantastic or fabulous. Other histories than the histories of the Old World were thus perfectly respectable. They were worthy to be set alongside those which came from the Bible, from Antiquity, from the Turks and from Renaissance Europe.

So, if we find the beginnings of a global history in the *Repertorio*, it is owed, paradoxically, to this amalgam of astronomy and astrology. The astronomical and astrological context provided an explanatory system of universal value, a code for reading applicable whatever the latitude and period, and a way of connecting up the histories of the peoples of the world. The Europeans did not have a monopoly, since other peoples, such as the Chinese, had 'great astrologers'.[39] The system was universal because it made it possible to interpret people's behaviour and hence the fate of societies all over the globe. Mathematics, astronomy and astrology came together in this supposedly 'scientific' reading of the world. It would be difficult today to follow our German down this path, even if we share with him one of the mainsprings of his perception of globality: belief in meteorological and astrological predictions. Is it not weather forecasts that are currently plunging the whole of humanity into the expectation of planetary disaster thanks to global warming? Heinrich Martin told his Mexican readers that the science of the astronomers made it possible to predict eclipses everywhere in the world, even in countries as yet unknown or reputed to be inaccessible. Conceived so as to be consulted in Mexico, his *lunario* was also presented as a universal tool: 'its method of use [enables it] to be employed in other parts of the world'.[40] In the sixteenth century this scientific and meteorological phase was another step towards world consciousness.

Other features are today more disconcerting. 'Global' history à la Heinrich Martin prioritized the great political and religious transformations because these upheavals prefigured the endgame that the Last Judgement would announce, 'the incomparable change of the universal Judgement'.[41] All astrologers like to speculate about the end of the world and this concern sometimes reveals more specific preoccupations. Heinrich Martin makes a particular point of evoking the 'destruction' of Christian Spain, as if this reminder was enough to send a shiver down the spine of his Spanish readers. This disaster had ended in the Islamization of a large part of the Peninsula. It had happened during the tyrannical reign of King Rodrigo, who had conceived the notion of opening up a palace in Toledo called the House of Hercules which was closed 'with many locks and padlocks'. The great men of the kingdom had explained to the king that opening this house would bring great misfortunes to the kingdom of Spain, and formally advised him not to implement his plan. Rodrigo had persisted, nevertheless, convinced that the building concealed treasures. The locks were forced and within was found a statue of Hercules which had in one hand the following inscription: 'I am Hercules the strong, he who conquered all Spain and killed Geryon who possessed it, and just as it is by me that Spain has been populated, so it is by you that it will be depopulated.' Beside the statue was a canvas painted with figures representing Arab knights, surrounded by a Greek inscription: it predicted what did not fail to happen, the conquest and destruction of Spain by the Moors.[42]

Should the Peninsula fear a new blow of fate? Should the tolling of the Aragonese bell tower be taken seriously? Was Heinrich Martin speaking in veiled terms of the end of Hapsburg Spain?

– 7 –

Islam at the Heart of the Monarchy

Spain, *nutrix mahometicae pravitatis*
Arnaud de Villeneuve, *De Mysterio cymbalorum*, 1301

The astrological preoccupations of Heinrich Martin would have been enough on their own to explain his particular interest in Islam and Turkey. With the exception of African slaves, only semi-converted to Christianity, and clandestinely arrived Moriscos, there were virtually no Muslims on the continent of America in the sixteenth century. Indeed it was the only part of the world that seemed to have escaped the grasp of Islam. The advance of the Turks in central Europe was hardly likely to strike fear into the elites of New Spain, protected as they were by the rampart of the Ocean. But this is to forget that these elites belonged to a monarchy whose peninsular heart could not ignore Islam, if only because of the close relations – of hatred and fascination, of familiarity, of exchanges and aversion –[1] that bound Iberian Christendom to the Muslim world. These centuries-old ties were still so strong that they fostered a real sense of guilt in the Spain of Charles V, where prophecies circulated recalling that the country 'had clad in iron and supported the evil sect of Mahomet and of the

Jews enemies of Jesus Christ',[2] and that it consequently deserved the punishment of God.

The Memory of *Al-Andalus*

In fact how could one evoke the history of the Iberian Peninsula without taking account of the centuries of Muslim domination and settlement and the long process by which the populations of Islamic origin had been converted, marginalized and eliminated? It was only in 1492 that the last Muslim kingdom in Spain had fallen, bringing to an end more than seven hundred years of political and military presence. And it had been a presence in the full sense of the term, not an occupation. As if nostalgic for it, the Anonymous Chronicler of Istanbul dwelled on this Andalusia of unsurpassed influence. Its artists and its navigators still lingered in the Muslim memory and this inhabitant of the shores of the Bosphorus was surprisingly familiar with this other Islam solidly implanted in the west of the Old World: 'The noble mosque of Cordova has become proverbial, because it is embellished and decorated with all sorts of gorgeous things and is unique in its beauty and perfection.'[3]

The Muslim presence was manifest in every sphere, but it had been first and foremost a human reality, tangible in the spaces where the two worlds had never ceased to confront and to mix with each other, even in the Christian territories. In the thirteenth century, when the Christian kingdoms were predominant in the Peninsula, they still retained their Muslim populations. For King Alphonso X of Castile, 'the Moors should live among the Christians in the same manner as . . . the Jews, observing their own law and causing no offence to ours'.[4] The Muslims who lived under Christian rule were given a particular name: *mudejares*, 'those who have been left behind'. In fact these conquered populations had been subject to all sorts of restrictions and often humiliations, varying according to the region or kingdom, but they had retained their mosques and their schools. And still, in the fourteenth and fifteenth centuries, the *mudejar* way of life permeated the whole of Castilian society, including its housing, furniture, clothing, fashions and cookery.[5]

This presence explains why, although the town of Lisbon had been restored to Christian hands in 1147, there were still two or three active mosques in the city in the fifteenth century, indicating that a Morisco population continued to live in Portugal. It was only in 1496, under pressure from his parents-in-law, the Catholic Kings, that King Manuel ordered the expulsion of the Moors from his kingdom. Those who preferred to remain in the country were required to convert and become *muladies*, or Moriscos.[6] Yet six years later, when Cardinal Cisneros in his turn expelled the Muslims from Castile, many of them moved to Portugal in the hope of finding more lenient conditions there.

The Iberian kingdoms were the only Christian lands to shelter formerly Muslim populations of any significance: in 1530 half the inhabitants of the kingdom of Granada, and in Valencia a third, were of Muslim origin. These people formed minorities which were often likened to a fifth column ready to receive assistance from the Turks or the Barbary states. Many more of them than is generally believed remained faithful to Islam. Ways of dressing, eating and dancing, ceremonies and rituals and a literature – *escritas aljamiadas* and *orações* – attest to the persistence of a singularity which the laws of Castile and Portugal struggled in vain to suppress.[7] Forcibly converted to Christianity, the Moriscos of Spain and Portugal were still able to keep alive, for almost a century, a large part of the Hispano-Muslim heritage. Observers made no mistake: 'they remained as Moorish as on the first day';[8] and an expert of the calibre of L. P. Harvey prefers to speak of Muslims, rather than Moriscos, so as to emphasize how deeply entrenched Islam was. It was not until the beginning of the seventeenth century, a few years after the appearance of the *Repertorio*, that the Moriscos were finally expelled from Spain.[9] Counter-Reformation Spain chose definitive separation as opposed to the uncertainties of medieval coexistence.

In the sixteenth century the Hispano-Muslim presence was still visible in the urban setting, in the agrarian landscape and irrigated crops and in the crafts, architecture and the decorative arts. Many mosques were turned into churches and many palaces and fortresses rebuilt by the Christians. The functions changed, the decor remained, and probably much more besides. The richness of *mudejar* art reveals the originality of the interchanges between Iberian and Muslim traditions and the porosity of the frontiers between Muslims, Jews and Christians. As with all artistic cross-fertilization, these interchanges involved judicious mixtures, involving technical combinations and symbolic transfers, but they remained dependent on the balance of power between the adversaries. But it was not only ways of doing things that were mutually influenced over the centuries, but also ideas and beliefs. More or less everywhere, even when they remained faithful to the Koran, the Morisco communities were forced to invent ways of life, or survival, which placed them between the Christian world and the Muslim world abroad, and which involved numerous coming togethers and superimpositions, to the great displeasure of the defenders of Catholic orthodoxy and purity of blood.

But the Muslim heritage was not always so physical; it was philosophical and scientific, too. Astronomy, cartography, the natural sciences, medicine and botany were all fields in which the Iberians, especially the Portuguese, appropriated Arabic science wholesale. They adopted measuring instruments like the *balestilha* (from *bilisti* meaning height), or cross-staff, they retained the use of the finger as a unit of calculation and they resorted to Arab maps and pilots. Vasco de Gama recruited Ahmad ibn Majîd. Knowledge of the sea drew on the *Secret of secrets* (or *Purity of purities*), wrongly taken to be a work of

Aristotle, but actually the Latin translation of an Arabic text, the *Sîr al-asrâr*,[10] itself derived from Sanskrit literature. Mesue was the apothecary par excellence and his works were published in Latin in the sixteenth century: *Textus Mesue* (1505) and *De re medica* (1531). The weights used by the apothecaries or *boticarios* were of Arab origin; in Portugal the *arrátel* continued in use until the eighteenth century.[11] One of the greatest Portuguese physicians of the sixteenth century, Garcia da Orta, constantly referred to the scholarship of the 'Arab doctors',[12] which he lost no opportunity to praise. University medicine followed the Persians, Rhazes and Avicenna, and read Hippocrates in the Arabo-Latin version, *Ad Almanzorem*.[13] This debt and this kinship have long been underestimated. To recognize them for what they are confronts us with a strange paradox. This profound immersion probably helped to distance Iberian science from the major developments inaugurated by the astronomy of Copernicus, the alchemy of Paracelsus and the *Nova anatomia* of Vesalius (1543). It was as if, by the sixteenth century, the contribution of Antiquity as revisited by the Muslims had become an intellectual millstone for the scholars of the Iberian Peninsula, who were unable to bring themselves to abandon Galen and Avicenna.

The heritage was also underlying where one might least expect it, in the writing of history,[14] in philosophical thinking and in Christian mysticism. The Hispanic Aristotelianism of the sixteenth century, as elsewhere in Europe, was dependent on the contribution of Averroes and Avicenna, by way of the twelfth-century Jewish thinker, Maimonides.[15] The mysticism of sixteenth-century Spain would be inconceivable without the contributions of the Jewish cabbala, but equally without those of Islamic gnosis.[16] The Muslim mystics like al-Ghazzali (Algazel) were not the forerunners, certainly, of John of the Cross, Teresa of Avila or Frei Thomé de Jesus, but the spiritual blossoming of the sixteenth century owed much to the centuries of Hispano-Muslim experience which had preceded it. The fact remains, too much closeness is a killer. The anti-Muslim polemic and Maurophobia fostered an attitude of rejection which destroyed most of these links. Educated Christians might have appreciated the astrology of Alî ibn al Ridjâl (Abenragel) and Abu-Mashar (Albumazar), but they were much less interested in the Arabic language,[17] and they frankly denied the existence of an original philosophical thought, even maintaining that it had been banned by Mahomet himself.

Nevertheless, the intellectual life of the Moriscos of Spain and Portugal did not die out completely in the sixteenth century. They lost the use of the Arabic language but they kept their alphabet to write the Spanish dialect (*romanço*) they spoke, so giving rise to the *aljamia* or *escrita aljamiada*.[18] In Spain, their brothers in Castile, Granada and Aragon transmitted or recopied works which were read throughout the sixteenth century. Religious writings, books of piety, legal commentary and, though less often, texts intended to entertain reveal the vitality of the clandestine cultures, echoes of which surface in the *Don Quixote* of Cervantes when the latter attributes authorship of his masterpiece to the Moorish writer Cid Hamete Benengali.[19]

Conquista and Reconquista

'One experiences innumerable regrets and as many griefs . . . at the idea that many hundreds of thousands of eminent Muslims, of great ulemas and of pious and just persons have been ruined at the hands of the contemptible Infidel', wrote the Anonymous Chronicler of Istanbul. The fall of the kingdom of Granada in 1492 traditionally marks the end of the *Reconquista*, and since this date is also that of the first voyage of Christopher Columbus, it is seen as marking the start of the American *Conquista*, too, as if Castile had providentially moved on from the battle against

Iberian Islam to the conquest of its planetary empire. Fate had ordered things remarkably well and contemporaries did not fail to establish the connection. Soon blessed by the pope, the principle of a sequence of *Reconquista* and *Conquista* speaks volumes as to the way in which Castilians associated maritime expansion and the age-old battle against the Muslims.[20]

The new venture still needed to be sacralized. The discovery of America was a sign sent by God to the Catholic Kings. The first and best interpreter of the New World remains Christopher Columbus, who transformed his maritime prowess by ascribing it universal significance. Had his 'discovery' not been predicted in the sacred texts? As, for example, in Psalm 19, which exalts Yahweh, the Sun of Justice: 'Their line is gone out through all the earth, and their words to the end of the world';[21] or Isaiah: 'For, behold, I create new heavens and a new earth . . . behold, I create Jerusalem'.[22] The Genoese Columbus was convinced that he was the celestial messenger mandated to announce the new heaven and the new earth described by St John (Revelation, 21,1), and that the Catholic Kings were the instruments chosen by God to preach the Gospel to the whole world. What had this to do with Islam? 'I have declared to your Highnesses that all the profit from my enterprise will be spent on the conquest of Jerusalem.' Columbus had an *idée fixe*: it was with gold from the Indies that the Spanish monarchs would be able to fulfil the prophecy of Joachim de Fiore and embark on the conquest of the Holy Places and rebuild Mount Zion.[23] The time would soon come for the conversion of the peoples of the earth.[24] The continuation of the crusade justified, therefore, the conquest and despoliation of the New World. The fate of America and the land of Islam were linked by 1492, even before the western isles had become the fourth part of the world.

But the *Conquista* did not bring the *Reconquista* to an end. As a prelude to his fourth voyage (1502–4), Columbus would like to have given assistance to the

Portuguese, besieged by the Moroccans in Arzila, some forty kilometres from Tangiers. The Aragon of King Ferdinand continued to play the Mediterranean card. Master of a Spain that was now a true frontier of Christendom, flushed with success after the war of Granada, king of Naples since 1504, Ferdinand the Catholic was firmly resolved to dominate the western Mediterranean. But his counsellor, Cardinal Francisco Jiménez de Cisneros, was also an ardent supporter of the idea of a resumption of the crusade. Cisneros preached the destruction of the Mahometan sect and already visualized himself in Jerusalem, administering the Eucharist to Ferdinand and his sons-in-law, Manuel of Portugal and Henry of England. In other periods, and if the cardinal had achieved his aims, the image would have spread all over the world. The actual results were more modest. Nevertheless, the Spanish seized Mers el-Kebir in 1505, Oran in 1509 and Bougie and Tripoli in 1510. Prophecies of Joachimite inspiration hailed Cisneros as the *pastor angelicus* appointed by God to crush Islam.[25] In the summer of 1511 Ferdinand was preparing to sail for Tunis when the war against France forced him to cut short his plans.[26] An atmosphere of messianic exaltation spread beyond the frontiers of Castile to affect other European milieus at the dawn of the Reformation. The rebellion of Luther was only a few years away.[27]

There were many more twists and turns in Spain's battle against Mediterranean Islam during the sixteenth century, as the confrontation spread to other parts of the world. In the first half of the century, at the head of an expanding empire, Suleiman the Magnificent emerged as the planetary rival of Charles V, to the point where the Turk came to supplant the Moor as chief object of European fears. The threats which hung over the Christian shores of the Mediterranean and central Europe – Hungary fell to the Turks in 1526, three years before the siege of Vienna – tormented the Christians of the Renaissance. Every humanist wrote a treatise on it: the Italian Paolo Giovio with his *Commentaries on Turkish Things*, the Valencian Luís

Vives with *Of the Condition of Life of Christians under the Turk* (1526) and *European Conflicts and Dialogue of the War against the* Turk (1527).[28]

Castilians, Aragonese and Portuguese might have united in their battle against Islam except that they all had different territorial objectives. Holding on to Tunis was crucial to assuring the security of Aragonese Italy (Naples and Sicily), but the interests of the Castilians lay more in crushing the Moors of Oran, Algiers and Bougie,[29] who plundered their coasts. The Portuguese, meanwhile, were still, as they had always been, primarily interested in Atlantic Morocco. The century was punctuated by resounding victories and defeats. Charles V launched two memorable attacks, one on Tunis, which was a success hailed throughout Christendom, the other on Algiers, which turned into a catastrophe. In 1571, the victory of Lepanto, given 'media coverage' as far away as Japan, created a momentary illusion that Catholic Christendom was capable of unity in order to crush the Turk; but it was never followed up. On the other hand, the great expedition to Morocco organized by Portugal in 1578 brought one disaster after another to Lisbon: the military rout of Ksar al-Kebîr, the decimation of the Lusitanian aristocracy, the death of King Sebastian and, soon after, in 1580, the union of the kingdom with the Spanish Crown.[30]

While discoveries and conquests continued overseas, the confrontation between the two camps dragged on in Christian Europe, which never managed to organize the final crusade which was still dreamed of by so many. This was largely attributable to the divisions of the Christian world, between Catholics and Protestants, but also between Catholic and Catholic, the king of France playing the Turkish card, Venice opting for neutrality. The idea of a crusade had not disappeared, but it was more as an ideal model of Christian unity in need of constant reinvention than as a plan of action that it lived on in the European imagination and oriented the way the world was seen. Viewed from Mexico, Lisbon, Goa or Naples, the battle of the European powers against the Turk was still regarded as one of the main-springs of the Christianization of the world. This is why to think Islam was necessarily also to think the world, whether the Old or the New.

One might conclude that if Islam had not existed, it would have been necessary to invent it. If only because it immediately legitimized the conquest of the Spanish Indies. From the outset, the Jerusalem of Columbus and Ferdinand appeared as the ultimate aim of the *Conquista* because it remained the lost heart of the Judeo-Christian world. What was it hoped for from the newly discovered lands if not that they would provide the wealth necessary to the recovery of the Holy Places, the conquest of Jerusalem and victory over Islam? American gold was heaven-sent to finance the final crusade, justifying on its own all the wars and despoliation. It was the same with the spices of Portuguese India. The Catholic Kings would become 'lords of the whole world'.[31] The legitimacy of the invasion of the New World might be a matter for debate in the sixteenth century, but the European theologians believed that the war against the Moors and the Turks was a just war because the latter had wrongfully occupied Christian territories. This was the opinion of Bartolomé de Las Casas in his *Apologética historia sumaria*.[32]

So it was possible to be as fiercely pro-Indian as anti-Morisco and anti-Muslim. By the end of the sixteenth century the anti-Morisco tendency, always virulent in Spain, had spread even to the West Indies. In his monu-mental chronicle, one of the great evangelists of Mexico, the Franciscan Jerónimo de Mendieta, repeated a predic-tion of his Catalan brother, Francesc Eiximenis, applying it to the inhabitants of the New World: if one wished to spare Spain new sufferings, 'great changes, upheavals and enmities', it was necessary to Christianize the Indians and prevent their destruction, and not only exterminate the Moors: 'let us put an end to this villainous people who by every means, with their Mahometan sect, should be expelled, destroyed and annihilated for ever and always'.[33]

The good Indian, by which we should understand the Christian Indian, thus became the anti-Moor or anti-Morisco par excellence, even if for other Europeans, more numerous by far, indigenous peoples and Muslims were equal in opprobrium.

'Batman' against Islam

The Portuguese were not to be outdone. In 1504 King Manuel's envoy to the pope, Duarte Galvão, pressed for the Church to preach war against the *Rumes* (the Turks) and the reconquest of Jerusalem.[34] This sacred enterprise monopolized the thoughts of King Manuel: 'The great king Manuel will take Jerusalem and Ismaêl and make the universal law prevail.'[35] The Portuguese of this period had become masters of the art of cultivating dreams and silver, messianic hopes and the hunt for spices.[36]

Many people in medieval Europe, particularly in the Iberian Peninsula, shared the belief that the conquest of the world and universal domination would be achieved only through the crushing of Islam. This was an old idea. In the Peninsula it dated back to at least the end of the thirteenth century, when the Valencian physician Arnaud de Villeneuve had denounced a Spain that was 'nurse to Mahometan depravity' (*nutrix mahometicae pravitatis*), and which would continue to be plagued by civil wars until the arrival of a 'Bat king' who would 'devour the mosquitoes' (the Moriscos), seize Africa, destroy the head of the Beast and receive the universal monarchy. Arnaud had not remained immune to the Joachimite prophecies which circulated within his order, and which were forever being taken up again, translated and fleshed out to suit the circumstances of the day.[37] This was how, in the course of the fourteenth century, the notion of a king of Aragon destined to seize the Holy Places took root. More than a century later, and nearly twenty years before the fall of

Granada, in 1473, Ferdinand the Catholic was in his turn identified with the famous Bat that would destroy Islam. After the capture of Oran, in 1509, it was Cardinal Cisneros who was elevated to the rank of champion of Christendom and hailed with the title of *pastor angelicus*, that mysterious person who would reform Christianity and get rid of Islam, once and for all.[38]

The rumblings scarcely died down with the end of the reign of Ferdinand the Catholic. Nor did the anti-Muslim voices. In 1515 a man from Osma lay dying in a hospital in Salamanca. He found the strength, nevertheless, to predict a series of misfortunes which he blamed on Islam: for 1517, a threat looming in the East, for 1518, a revolt of the Muslims of Granada, for the year after that, the arrival of the Turk in Rome, which would put the pope to flight.[39] Uprisings of the great, the loss of Spain, bloody battles, the fulfilment of the prophecies of Jeremiah – the beginning of the reign of the future Charles V threatened to be especially troubled. In 1520 the uprising of the *Comunidades* against the young emperor gave credence to the mysterious prophet from Osma.

In this anti-Muslim atmosphere, the wildest rumours circulated. Some dreamed of 'cleansing' Spain of all its Moors, who would be expelled to the other shore of the Mediterranean, before the Christians embarked on the conquest of Jerusalem by way of North Africa and Alexandria.[40] The predictions of a cobbler from Trancoso, in the Portuguese province of Beira Alta, spread among the common people and the clergy. This man, who had been born around 1500 and was called Gonçalo Andres Bandarra, preached the arrival of the *Encoberto* ['The hidden one'], 'king of the sea routes and their riches', a mysterious sovereign of the Last Days who would fight against and crush Islam. 'Everyone will believe that the anointed saviour has arrived'.[41] He was taken to be prophesying what many hoped for, 'the ruin of the Ottoman Empire, the end of the law of *Mafoma* and the destruction of the house of Mecca':[42]

I have seen a great lion run
And make his journey
And take in passing
The savage pig
. . .
The moon will fall from on high
According to what one sees in her,
Just like those who are with her.

The texts are cryptic but contemporaries were in no doubt that the 'savage pig' or the 'king of Salem' to whom Bandarra referred could only be the Turk.[43]

In other circles the figure of the emperor Charles V also crystallized many hopes. From ordinary people to educated elites, and from Spain to the New World, the preparations for the expedition against Algiers (1541) set off a wave of messianic enthusiasm around the person of the sovereign, who was hailed as Emperor of the Last Days, he who would complete the reconquest of the Holy Places and receive the universal monarchy.[44] When the expedition turned into a disaster, these hopes regrouped and searched for other outlets.

Not all the defeats led to a lessening of zeal. The Portuguese rout in Morocco, in 1578, gave renewed fervour to the messianic dream. The death of King Sebastian during the defeat of Kasr al-Kebîr reactivated the link between crusade, messianic hopes and the battle against Islam. This gave birth to Sebastianism, which was still alive in twentieth-century Brazil. It primarily consisted of predictions foretelling the return of the dead king.[45] Sebastian would save Portugal from Castilian domination and found the fifth empire of the world. Politically, Sebastianism was a reaction to the turmoil caused by the African defeat, which had allowed Philip II to seize the Portuguese Crown and seal the union of the two empires. It condensed a range of popular beliefs and political designs around the theme of the dead king. Many were persuaded that the *Encoberto* foretold by Bandarra was the King Sebastian whose return seemed imminent. The unhappy sovereign was not dead, but roaming the world, fighting the Turks, while awaiting the day when he would recover his kingdom.[46] Defeated by the Muslims in 1578, the dead king would soon show himself and take his revenge. Meanwhile, his reappearances made news, and these false Sebastians rated a mention in the chronology of Heinrich Martin: 'In this same year [1585], two kings rose up in Portugal, both had been hermits who each passed himself off as Don Sebastian, although one was the son of a weaver and the other the son of a stone-cutter; the latter was hanged and the former sent to the galleys.'[47]

On the Muslim side too, events took an apocalyptic turn. Soon after Kasr al-Kebîr, some Moors circulated texts in Arabic characters that were full of 'predictions of the fall of the House of St Peter and St Paul'.[48] Some Portuguese Moriscos, in contrast, looked forward to the return of the unfortunate Sebastian and imagined that the hidden king was the *mahdî* who would rid them of the Castilian king.[49]

Destruction and Restoration

These hopes and dreams were all the more vivid and deep-rooted in that Islam was very far from being an exotic fantasy or relic from the past for the Christians of Spain. Seized in coastal raids or captured at sea, many of them risked long years of slavery in Algiers, Tunis, Morocco or even Istanbul. Having survived the battle of Lepanto, Miguel de Cervantes endured five hard years of this 'forced tourism', on which he drew to write a famous episode of *Don Quixote* and some comedies such as *The Baths of Algiers*. It was in circumstances such as these that many Spaniards had physical and psychological experience of the condition of slave.

As noted above, Islam was still present in the Peninsula itself. It was embodied in numerous Morisco communities which had been forcibly converted and which were suspected of being ready to seek the assistance of the Moors of Africa or the Turks. When, in 1568, the Moriscos of Granada chose the path of rebellion, the fear of a fifth column was in everybody's mind. Not entirely without reason, because the rebels were in contact with the Turks of Algiers and Istanbul,[50] and even received the support of Turkish auxiliaries infiltrated via the coasts. The Moriscos of Granada were crushed in 1571, but the presence of Muslims in the Peninsula would long continue to be a source of anxiety, giving rise to the wildest of fears. To be rid of them, solutions as horrifying as collective drowning or deportation to the ice fields of Newfoundland appear to have been contemplated in the 1580s: 'They will die out there completely, especially if the adult and young males are castrated and the women [are sterilized].'[51] The Moriscos escaped this 'final solution', but not expulsion. It was in 1609, under Philip III, that all Moriscos were driven out of the kingdoms of Spain. The operation, which took several years and required considerable resources, brought to an end many centuries of coexistence and conflict, but the Muslim threat continued to hang over the Christian coasts. For a long time to come, *Moros* and Turks who scoured the seas would reduce sailors, peasants and fishermen from Christian villages to slavery; and vice-versa.

There remained the world scene, inseparable from local realities. In North Africa, in East Africa, from Mozambique to the Red Sea, in India, in the Moluccas and in the Philippines, everywhere, or almost, Iberians and Muslims came face to face. Not only a religious rival, but also a political and commercial rival, Islam was that universal opposite that was generally feared and that had been known for a very long time. Things would have been simple if, paradoxically, the worst enemies of the monarchy had not been other Christians, Catholics in France and heretics in Germany, England and Holland, that is, new adversaries who proved a good deal more harmful than the Turks in the short run and, in the long run, all-round victors.[52]

Near or far, fantasy and reality, at once incarnation of evil and 'scourge of God',[53] Islam played a singularly ambiguous role. Architect or object of destruction? It might equally well be the providential hand which fell on the bad Christians or the target of an impatiently-awaited annihilation. The Muslim invasion of the Peninsula had come, in its own day, to punish the sins of King Rodrigo. Was there not a risk that the Muslim conquest might be repeated? When Bartolomé de Las Casas denounced the 'destruction of the Indies', his formulation went beyond the idea of simple material devastation. It revived memories of the invasion which had ruined Christian Spain; even more, however, it left hanging the threat of a new destruction, this time at the hands of the Turks:

> Spain has been destroyed once by the Moors and although it is said that it was on account of the sin of King Rodrigo who violated the daughter of the count Don Julian, it would be better to believe it was on account of the sins of the whole people and the evils and the damage caused to their fellow men . . . I have heard many people say: 'May it please God not to destroy Spain for all the evils that they say have been committed in the Indies!'[54]

The leitmotiv of destruction or loss was an Iberian obsession. All through the sixteenth century and still in the seventeenth, 'the spectre of the recurrence of the "destruction of Spain" continued to haunt certain people . . .'. At the time of the revolt of the *Comunidades* against Charles V, a rumour had circulated that God was punishing the laxity of the rich towards the Jews and the Moors by sending the anti-Christ and by causing a new destruction of Spain. Suggested in Las Casas, the destruction of Spain was explicitly predicted by some Moriscos in the Peninsula: 'In a book of St Isidore we find that the Turk was to conquer all this land and that he would bring with him vermin never seen or heard-of in these parts.'[55] Foolhardy visionaries scoured the Spain of Philip II and Philip III predicting 'the extinction of the House of Austria and the restorative coming of a new David on the throne of Spain'.[56] Without going to such extremes, by dint of evoking the theme of a necessary restoration of Spain, observers could instil the idea that a destruction was under way.[57]

Back to Mexico

This fear belonged as much to the old theory of the succession of empires as to the history of Spain or the Indies. In the *Repertorio*, the words 'destruction' and 'perdition' abound, and they are explicitly associated with the Ottoman Empire.[58] They are also accompanied by considerations whose banality cannot mask the insidious ambiguity:

> Temporal states develop in such a way that they never stay in the same condition; on the contrary, they rise and fall, grow and diminish each in proportion as do all the other things of the world and each has its term and its limit, fixed by divine providence . . . when a kingdom or a monarchy or some state has reached the peak of its grandeur, which is visible when it ceases to grow and to expand, then it begins to decline.

Giovanni Botero had said very much the same thing a few years earlier in his *The Reason of State*: it is far more difficult for a prince to keep his kingdom than to expand it.

These considerations might equally well apply to a Catholic monarchy which 'has reached the peak of its grandeur'. But it would have been risky for a faithful servant of the king and the Inquisition to say such a thing openly in Mexico. Reading between the lines of the *Repertorio*, one is led to wonder if, by so insistently referring to the fall of the Ottoman Empire, and by expatiating on the weakness of empires, Heinrich Martin may have been seeking to make his readers share the unease then provoked by the fate of the Spanish Crown. The interminable war against Holland, the consolidation of France and the financial problems were ominous signs. Martin followed world events too closely not to be aware of this. In his heart of hearts, and in his readers' hearts too, was the Turkish Empire not the mirror of the Spanish monarchy? In which case, by a simple inversion of things, the Ottoman threat became the sword of Damocles suspended over the Spanish Crown; and the bell tower of the Ebro never ceased to reverberate in troubled minds.

– 8 –

Islam in the New World

Going by certain rites and customs of these Indians [of Mexico], some Spaniards consider and say that they are of the stock of the Moors.

Motolinía, *Memoriales*

What did Islam and the Turks represent for the inhabitants of Mexico? Settled thousands of miles away from any Muslim lands, these were people who had spent, and would spend, most of their lives far removed from any danger. For them, Islam was both a faceless and an unlikely enemy, since it presented no threat, direct or indirect, near or far, to this part of the world.[1] If we except, that is, the appeals for conquest launched by the Anonymous Chronicler of Istanbul, which were never followed up. No more than was an Anglo-Moroccan project for the invasion of Spanish America. Elizabeth I, at the very beginning of the seventeenth century, had entered into talks with the sultan of Morocco with a view to mounting a programme of conquest and colonization; it was to rely on African soldiers, who were reckoned to be better able to withstand the heat of the tropics.[2]

In fact, though the Spanish Crown had prohibited all emigration to the West Indies by Moriscos, even for the purpose of developing the raising of silkworms,[3] some members of these communities and some Spaniards of Morisco descent managed to slip through the net.[4] Others ended up in the New World against their will. Turkish and Moorish slaves served in the Caribbean.[5] Blacks deported from Africa had inevitably introduced syncretic beliefs, practices and objects of Muslim origin. The magic amulets, or *bolsas de mandinga*, found in Brazil reveal transmissions that should not be underestimated.[6] But there was nothing resembling a public presence, open and proselytizing. Unlike the Judaizers and the Protestants, the Moriscos provided few clients for the Inquisition of the Indies. Nor had anything of the atmosphere of permanent and bitter polemic prevailing between Moriscos and Christians in the Peninsula spread to the New World.[7]

Moors in the Landscape

Paradoxically, that Islam had a certain presence in the New World was primarily due to the way that the invading Christians had brought a little of Muslim Spain with them as they arrived. Conquerors and colonists introduced the arts and the customs with which the Mudejar world had familiarized them. Many traces of this are found in the colonial architecture and on the walls of the cloisters of Mexico City, where paradisal vegetation still celebrates the encounter of the Amerindians of the New World with the ornamental profusion that had developed in Arabo-Christian lands a few centuries earlier.[8] The first viceroy of Mexico, Antonio de Mendoza, was the son of the count of Tendilla, the man given responsibility by the Catholic kings for the government and 'integration' of the kingdom of Granada after its reconquest.[9] The experience accumulated in daily contact with the Muslims of Spain would stand the ruler of Mexico in good stead.

Did the conquistadors originally imagine a Muslim America? From the very first contacts, Spaniards seeking to comprehend the strangeness of Mexico compared it to what they knew best, projecting onto the new lands what they knew, or thought they knew, about the Muslim world, a world to which they had been so close in space and time.[10] Thus the Mexico of the conquest was often seen as looking like Africa or Muslim Spain. In 1517 the first large agglomeration discovered on the coast of Yucatan was given the name 'El Gran Cairo', probably because up to this date the capital of the Mamelukes had filled every traveller with admiration:[11] 'this united and compact city . . . three times as large as Paris and five times more populous'.[12] Three years later, the descriptions of Tlaxcala and Cholula left by Cortés in his second *Carta de relación* are as seen through the prism of Granada. The town of Tlaxcala 'is much larger than that of Granada and much stronger, with equally good buildings and many more people than had Granada at the time of its conquest, and it is much better supplied with local produce'. Its inhabitants are 'reasonable and orderly people, superior to the best one finds in Africa'. Those of Cholula, another prestigious Indian city, have an African air: 'the notables wear the burnoose over their garments, but different from those of Africa because they have openings for the hands, but in their manufacture, their material and their repair, they are truly the same'. The urban landscape was in keeping. Cortés said, again of Cholula: 'I counted from the top of one mosque four hundred and twenty towers in this city and they are all of mosques.' Mexico City, too, seemed to be covered with mosques.[13] The tax collectors of Moctezuma became his 'almojarifes', and the granaries where the tributes were stored became 'alholíes'.[14]

Further contact soon dispelled the confusion, but the Spanish retained the habit of making such associations every time they found themselves faced with new populations. As, for example, with the Chichimecs, the nomadic Indians of the frontier, who rebelled against colonial rule and Christianization, and the speed of whose attacks and rapidly-acquired mastery of the horse made them into 'alarabs'.[15] In the same spirit, at the end of the century, the rebellion of the Araucans of Chile was compared to the revolt of the Moriscos of Spain in 1568. Later, during his expedition, Coronado likened the peoples of the far north of New Spain to Turks.[16] In Brazil, the eastern and Muslim references were even more visibly and durably apparent. The Mamelukes of Egypt gave their name to the children born of Portuguese fathers and Indian mothers, the *mamelucos*; they had proved so pitiless in hunting down the Indians that they were likened to the mercenaries of Cairo legendary for their cruelty and aggression. The name seems to have persisted throughout the colonial period, as the sources still mention the presence of *mamelucos* as slaves in the Amazonia of the eighteenth century.[17]

America was connected to Islam by something even deeper, bound up with the very nature of the first relations established by the Castilians with the New World, when they had linked reconquest and conquest. The medieval *Reconquista* had been a holy war conducted by Christians against the Infidel. A crusade on Iberian territory, it was the counterpart of the Islamic jihad, 'motive force of the Almorávides'.[18] The *Conquista* of America was also claimed as a just war, dedicated to converting the rebellious Indians to Christianity. Even if it was not overtly presented as a holy war, it inextricably associated war and religion.[19] There are many examples of this. The likening of the Indians to the Moors, and the *Conquista* to a crusade, explains the introduction of the cult of Santiago Matamoros (St James the Moor-Slayer) to the New World. St James had appeared on a white horse at the battle of Clavijo, in 822, and his miraculous intervention had saved the troops of Ramiro, king of Aragon, from the Muslim assaults. The miracle was subsequently repeated in the Iberian Peninsula, then on the other side of the Ocean, where it was Americanized.[20] In 1535, in the middle of the invasion of Peru, the apostle of the *Reconquista* had appeared at Cuzco. The town was then under siege from the Indians and the conquistadors had reacted to this desperate situation by beseeching the assistance of the saint. St James had answered their prayers. On a tremendous thunderbolt, and accompanied by a flash of lightning which struck the Indian fortress of Sacsahuaman, he descended from the skies. The Spanish immediately recognized their saviour, whereas the horrified Indians thought it was their god Illapa who had fallen from the sky to chastise them. Brandishing his sword, the saint rode a white horse adorned with many little bells. He quickly forced the Indians to lift the siege and gave victory to the conquistadors. Once he had become the patron saint of the town of Cuzco, St James changed his name from Matamoros to one that was more appropriate to the local context, Mataindios (Indian-Slayer). Paintings hanging in the cathedral of Cuzco and other churches in the country have immortalized the prodigy by showing a triumphant saint engaged in massacring all the Indians who came within his reach.[21] Power of the horse and the sword, supernatural power come from the sky, force of arms compared to thunder: Spanish America appropriated the patron of the Iberian *Reconquista*, although the pre-eminence of the apostleship of St James was by no means unanimously accepted on the Peninsula itself.

Crusading in the Sierra

In both Peru and Mexico, the Indians, once defeated, were supposed to join the camp of the victors. From the idolaters they had been, they became Christians, with all the obligations conversion implied, namely obedience to the Spanish clergy, the practice of monogamy, denunciation of Judaizers, idolaters and heretics and fighting Muslims. All this was in accord with both the spirit and the letter of the pontifical bulls which had handed a large part of the globe to the Iberians.

It is hardly surprising that, in the early days of colonization, some of the missionaries tried to win the Indians over to the idea of crusade. They needed to instil into them the urgency of the fight against the *Moros*, make it clear who was their real enemy and pass on the host of fears and fantasies the Iberians nurtured concerning Islam. The project today seems highly fanciful, so deeply is the idea of crusade bound up with heritages and even more with a conception of religion and holy war which had their roots in a very different history than that of America.

It is probably in Mexico that one can follow most closely the stages in this 'colonization of the imaginary', part of a mimetic re-creation. The Spanish did not arrive empty-handed. Scarcely had they landed before they introduced practices long familiar in the Peninsula: parades, simulated fights and festive jousts mimicking the battles between Moors and Christians. By 1524, and perhaps earlier, on his way to Nicaragua, Cortés was welcomed at Coatzalcoalcos by festivities of this type.[22] The Indians, defeated or allies, without yet much understanding of the Christian faith, were content to be spectators at these exotic celebrations. At best, they equated them with the ritual battles which took place within their own ranks during religious sacrifices and feasts. As the conquerors became established and as evangelization progressed, more ambitious projects appeared. In 1539 the celebration of the Truce of Nice between Charles V and Francis I was the pretext for sumptuous festivities in the Mexican capital. It was an opportunity for an amazing spectacle in which scenes from the Crusades were staged in the middle of Mexico City, and Christians of the island of Rhodes were to be seen fighting against the Turks. The combatants were conquistadors in disguise, some as knights of St John of Jerusalem, others as Turks. The Indians who made up the majority of the audience had also provided the manpower to construct the scenery and the ships mounted on wheels that manoeuvred round the main square. Some of them also appeared perched on these caricatures of vessels, disguised as Dominicans and prosaically occupied fishing or plucking chickens.

The spectacle delighted the crowds of the Mexican capital and persuaded their perennial rivals, the Indians of Tlaxcala, to stage an even more grandiose performance. The context is worth recalling. The city of Tlaxcala had suffered less than others from the Spanish invasion because it had chosen the right side at the time of the Conquest, that is, the side of the conquistadors. As the Tlaxcalans had continued to be exemplary collaborators, the Franciscans who had converted them decided to give them their support. Tlaxcala would present a 'conquest of Jerusalem' that would be a worthy competitor to the celebration in Mexico City. At stake was not only the prestige of the 'imperial city' of Tlaxcala but the reputation of the mendicant order and also the boost that would be given to the Christianization of the population. On a stage the size of four football pitches, with thousands of extras and settings to make the capital green with envy, there appeared principal characters the like of which had never been seen before: the pope, the cardinals, the emperor, the 'sultan of Babylon', the viceroy of Mexico, Hernán Cortés, his lieutenant Pedro de Alvarado and many others. The Indians of Tlaxcala succeeded in dazzling their contemporaries. Spaniards, Europeans and Indians of New Spain, the Caribbean and Peru – all played by Tlaxcalans, of course – spent several days doing battle with the forces of the Sultan, which included Moors, Jews and Syrians. Christian Europe and the New World took on the Muslims and recaptured Jerusalem. The Sultan was forced to acknowledge defeat and accept baptism. The spectacle was not without its anachronisms. The leader of the Muslims was called the 'great sultan of Babylon', that is, of Cairo, when the capital of the Mamelukes had already been under Ottoman rule for twenty years. The Islamic soldiers were *Moros*, that is, Moors, not *Turcos*. The anachronisms only heightened the allegorical dimension of the Tlaxcalan production. There was another consequence, however. It was the medieval East of crusading and Franciscan millenarianism that was recreated on Indian soil. As regards Islam, the broad mass of America thus lagged behind Mexico City, which was better informed and which had staged, at a distance, the confrontation with the Turks in the eastern Mediterranean.[23] This twofold portrait of Islam, which juxtaposed the political and up-to-date eye of a western capital and the outdated gaze of the indigenous country-side, had a long future ahead of it. As did the confusions to which it gave rise. The Indians of Tlaxcala, caught up in a history that was not their own, like many peoples in the world today, were unaware that they were old-fashioned and that their fellows in Mexico City were modern!

This deployment of 'American' troops – extras cos-tumed as Peruvians and Indians from the Caribbean fought alongside the Mexicans – in a theatrical setting that depicted the Middle East is disturbing. Less because it could evoke recent events than in the way in which the Indians of the whole continent became full-blown protag-onists in the battle against Islam. The Indians played at being and acted being crusaders; they practised attacking what was destined to become their prime objective, the town of Jerusalem, and their chosen target, the Muslim forces. They gained familiarity with their new allies, Germans, Italians, Romans, French and Hungarians, who reinforced the Spanish. The Tlaxcalan 'production' was based on a basic but effective geopolitics. Before the eyes of the indigenous crowds it opposed goodies and baddies, the 'allies' (Indian America and imperial Europe) and the Moors, the Turks and the Jews, imparting maximum clarity to the presentation; positions, emblems and cos-tumes provided the essential reference points. Whereas Rhodes and the Mediterranean had been the backdrop to the celebration in Mexico City, in Tlaxcala the site of the battles was closer to that described in the stories of pilg-rims to the Holy Land, Judea, Syria and Damascus. But Jerusalem would remain in Indian eyes a name on a paste-board fortification, unlike the town of Rhodes, which the artisans of the Mexican capital had striven to reproduce with a clear concern for realism – '*tan al natural*' – which

may be explained by the presence in the city of many conquistadors originally from the Aegean.[24] At Tlaxcala,
words took precedence over local colour. Long harangues
in Nahuatl commented on the action, directed the movements of the army and drummed in the values of crusading
and Christianity.

In the medium term, the success of these ventures –
Mexico City and Tlaxcala – was shown by the proliferation of festivals of *Moros y Cristianos* in the indigenous
villages of Mexico and the Philippines. At the end of the
century, the town of Mexico even embarked on a remake
of the battle of Rhodes, organizing the defence against the
Turks of a castle built near the lagoon.[25] The success of
these festivities is still visible today, even if the celebrations
have long lost their original meaning and the *Moros* frequently changed their identity. A virtual enemy lends itself
to endless recycling. Since the end of the nineteenth century,
the Moors of the crusade have often been replaced by the
Zouaves of Napoleon III, unhappy aggressors against an
independent and republican Mexico, and the crescent has
given way to the Tricolour of the invaders.[26]

In this first half of the sixteenth century, Islam Tlaxcala-
style served the monks well. It allowed them to defend
their policy of evangelization, demonstrate the mass
support of the indigenous populations and rehearse their
eschatological preoccupations. The 'fall of Jerusalem' was
meant to be both anticipation and acceleration of an imminent history. For the Franciscan Motolinía, 'the conquest
of Jerusalem' was a spectacle supposed to be a stage-
rendering of the near future. 'May God accomplish this
prediction in our own day',[27] he exclaimed in a letter to
the emperor. In organizing the representation on Tlaxcalan soil of the messianic and millenarian scenario of the
capture of the Holy Places, Motolinía assigned the Indians
and America their own place in the great eschatological
game, that is, on the planetary chessboard; a place that
must necessarily be achieved through the crushing of
Islam.[28] What if the Indians really were the descendents of

the Lost Tribes of Israel, and if they had reappeared so as
to mark the proximity of the End of Days?[29] Was the
Tlaxcalan celebration not fulfilling the programme
announced in a prophecy which Pope Leo X had sent to
King Ferdinand the Catholic: 'This great king Don
Carlos . . . will cross the sea with a large army, he will
subjugate the Chaldeans and destroy the Grand Turk and
the Palestinians, the Khan and the barbarians and then
seize the holy house of Jerusalem . . . he will be lord of
almost the whole world.'[30] Events in America put flesh on
the bones of the prophecy.[31] In enacting the capture of
Jerusalem in the middle of Mexico, the Indians were has-
tening the course of History. Every simulation was already
in part a fulfilment. It introduced an intermediate stage
between febrile expectancy and taking action. This is what
the monks must have felt and this is how they endeavoured
to manipulate history and the Indians. As for the indigenous peoples, they lived this experience all the more
intensely in that they were not simply 'actors' in the European sense; for these people, scarcely emerged from pre-
Hispanic celebrations, the incarnation to which they were
invited was probably more than simply a representation.
The virtual met the real, just as, in the past, the image-
ixiptla of the god had been god himself.

The Turks to the Rescue of America

So, by way of the Moors, the Turks made their appearance
on the Mexican scene in the course of the 1530s. They
were not forgotten in the second half of the century. The
celebration of the victory of Lepanto (1571) left traces in
the colonial theatre and in the indigenous codices and
writings. The Turk in the *colóquio* of the Battle of Lepanto
was heard lamenting his defeat before the public of Mexico
City in a pidgin French that was supposed to add local
colour.[32] Another sensational event, the massacre of the
Christians of Tunis in 1574, attributed to the troops of

Selîm II, inspired a stage play performed in the same city scarcely a year later at the Colegio Máximo de San Pedro y San Pablo.

But the Turks were also the scourge of God. Millenarian scenarios are tricky to exploit. They can at any moment backfire on the established authority, if they fail at some point to meet the expectations of the faithful or of Heaven. Christian Spain had already, in the past, been punished and destroyed by the Muslims. Why not go on to imagine that, one day soon, not only the Peninsula and the whole of Europe would be annihilated, but that America might serve as a sanctuary for those Christians spared by the destruction of the Old World? The history of the Church was favourable to such an idea. Since its origins, like the sun, it had been in constant motion in a westerly direction, from Jerusalem to Rome, and from Rome, who knows, perhaps to the New World? Time and space were super-imposed: 'And as in the beginning the Church flourished in the East which was the beginning of the world, it is right that now, at the end of the centuries, it should flourish in the West which is the end of the world.'[33]

These ideas were certainly circulating in New Spain and Peru, but their gravity demanded a discretion that means only very rare sources enable us to penetrate it today. In April 1578 the tribunal of the Inquisition of Lima sentenced the Dominican Francisco de la Cruz to the stake. Three times, this important personage, rector of the university of Lima and a significant player in the capital's social scene, had gone beyond the point of no return. Not only had this theologian repeated the attacks made by Bartolomé de Las Casas on the colonial system and incurred the anger of the viceroy of Peru, but he was accused of developing messianic and millenarian ideas with subversive undertones. His confession before the tribunal, which earned him his death in the flames, reveals how he imagined the role of Turkey vis-à-vis America and how he conceived the world and, in particular, the New World. Francisco de la Cruz expected to become king of Peru,

pope and even king of Israel because he believed that the
Indians were descended from the Jewish tribes that had
long been presumed lost. The throne of St Peter would rise
up in the New Jerusalem (Lima) and remain there at least
a thousand years. Peru would split off from the Peninsula
all the more easily in that Rome and Spain were to be
annihilated as the price of their sins: 'God wishes to destroy
Europe by the hand of the Turk.' It was for the Ottoman
Empire to do the dirty work by capturing the pope and
attacking Italy, France and Spain. In forty-two days European Christendom would be razed from the face of the
earth. At which point, maritime connections with the Old
World would cease and, along with them, any form of
relationship with the European peoples. An isolationist
vision, 'anti-globalist' before the term, tinged with a large
dose of pacifism, the discourse of this Dominican
propelled America to the forefront of the historical stage
while at the same time detaching it from the Euro-
Ottoman pairing.

The sources for this message come as no surprise: the
Apocalypse of John, the prophecies of the Old Testament,
Daniel, Abdias, Habakkuk, Isaiah and Ezekiel, interspersed
with Jewish and astrological references. More original was
the backing sought from among the Indians of Peru; the
indigenous belief in the inversion of the world, the
Pachacuti, confirmed de la Cruz in his conviction of the
ineluctable nature of the disturbances which lay ahead.
Heinrich Martin would later use local traditions in a
similar fashion to give additional weight to prophecy.

The wild Utopia of Francisco de la Cruz was a damp
squib. What survived was this premonition of independ-
ence, together with a transfer of Christendom to the Indies,
already nascent in the writings of Las Casas. The America
of Francisco de la Cruz was an America where every
prophecy was fulfilled. Not only a new 'promised land'
but a sanctuary for those who escaped the hand of the
Turk and Islam,[34] the New World awaited only the Puritans of the seventeenth century for the millenarian wave

to be set in motion once again. In any case, a decisive step had been taken in Lima as regards the 'conquest of Jerusalem'. The forces of the New World had ceased to be the preferred ally against the *Moros*, becoming instead the last recourse of the planet.[35]

The Renaissance Triangle

It was not only the Spanish Franciscans and Dominicans who were bowled over by the youth of a continent miraculously preserved from Islam. Others were affected, too, chief among them the English Protestants;[36] and among the heretics of London and Plymouth, too, the relationship with America was mediated through Islam.

The English of the Renaissance were not content with playing 'Moors and Christians' in lavish jousts on English soil; the image of Islam also haunted the parts of America they managed to seize from the Catholic monarchy. With them, the triangular relationship that was emerging between the lands of Islam, Europe and America took a new turn:[37] it added a new partner. In the last decades of the sixteenth century, an ever-larger number of the subjects of Queen Elizabeth experienced life not only in Indian America but in the Muslim Mediterranean, too. It seems, even, that many of them began by preferring this nearer and more familiar Mediterranean to the New World; it was more attractive to adventurers and less perilous than the unfathomable depths of the Ocean or the wild wastes on the other side of the Atlantic. Admittedly, with the exception of the Turkish or African slaves liberated during their raids in the Caribbean, the English did not encounter Muslims in America, but the Amerindian world seemed to them even more disquieting, wholly given over to the devil and peopled by immoral beings who rejected the revelations of Scripture.[38] At a very early stage, the indigenous societies they came into contact with became mirrors which reflected sinister glimpses of Islam. Moors and

Indians came to be confused even in the finest minds. The same fears and the same prejudices explain why the figure of the Muslim came gradually to be superimposed on that of the American Indian. They fantasized about the sodomy of the Indians just as they did about that of the Turks. They despised the abominable way of life of both. They spoke contemptuously of those Europeans who became renegades in the Maghreb or Virginia and ended up being Islamized or Indianized. Like the Spanish rivals they detested, and with an equal lack of scruple, some English began to laud the just war against the Indian and the holy war against Islam.

Yet the Indians were not quite the same as the Moors. Whereas the Indians of America let themselves be crushed and exterminated, the Barbary states and the Turks, now and for a long time to come, put up a hard fight. Was the New England destined to become the British Palestine? As London began to supplant Seville and Lisbon, North America took on the character of a promised land reserved for a chosen people; a people chosen by God to build 'Jerusalem in Virginia'.[39] The eschatological hopes which had originated in Mexico and peaked in Peru resurfaced in the wake of the English settlers; this time, however, the indigenous peoples were wholly excluded, rather than playing an integral role. In the Europe/America/Islam triangle, the American pole was now emptied of its autochthonous population. The Indians became 'Moors' to be crushed in order to gain this promised land in which the Puritans would build their city of Salem. The roles seemed interchangeable: the Indians were the Moors and the Moors Indians. The English in their turn, on the basis of their relations with the Indian populations of north-west America, developed a colonizing discourse which they would later, in the eighteenth century, apply to the Muslim states. One colonization leads to another. The predatory experience they acquired in America augured well for their future in the Muslim East. The British were encouraged by it to cast covetous glances at the Maghreb, proposing new forms of colonization which would be systematically implemented in the Age of Enlightenment.[40]

So we see re-form once again that 'Renaissance triangle' which indissolubly linked the lands of Islam and America to a triumphant and Christian Europe, Catholic or Protestant. It is a triangle which may be surprising today, it is so much at odds with our narrow view of the past. Yet how can we understand the curiosity of Heinrich Martin or the Anonymous Chronicler of Istanbul unless we locate them in a wider context which transcends the Iberian and Turkish worlds? The global context is self evident. The Spaniards and Portuguese who crossed the Ocean had not forgotten that, over the centuries, their relationship to the other had been built in the face of Islam, but also thanks to Islam, by the sword and exchanges of every type. For many of them, lived experience was more potent than memory in bringing the Barbary coasts closer to the coasts of the New World. Did not Miguel de Cervantes, a soldier who had experienced slavery and Islam in the penal colonies of Algiers, subsequently seek to emigrate to America? Cervantes was rejected, but how many others travelled from the Barbary coasts to those of Vera Cruz or Cartagena? Nor were the Iberians the only ones to make this journey – English, Italians, Dutch and French did so too. All through the sixteenth century multiple links, physical, emotional, real and virtual, were forged between the lands of Islam and the lands of America.

America/Islam/Europe: this is a triangle in which the Muslim viewpoint still largely eludes us. How did the Muslim slaves who landed up in the Caribbean perceive the Indian populations, forming in their turn other, more secret relationships between America, Islamic Africa and the Mediterranean? One wonders also about those Barbary state vessels which scoured the Atlantic in search of rich prey on its way back from the Indies. Well into the seventeenth century, the Portuguese Jesuit António Vieira still feared these attacks, which endangered relations between Brazil and the rest of the world. The Turks of Istanbul were not indifferent to this planetary dimension. The unpleasant way in which *Moros* and Indians came to be confused in the European gaze does not mean, as we have seen, that the Anonymous Chronicler of Istanbul would have been any more sensitive to the fate of the Amerindian populations. As seen from the shores of the Bosphorus, the cannibalistic and idolatrous Indians were little better than the Christians, and the Christians were no less than Infidel. The views of both intersected, were superimposed, coincided or clashed in the oceanic and planetary spaces that were coveted by both Christians and Muslims. America/ Europe/Islam – or, if preferred New World/Latin Christendom/African and Asian Islam. This was enough for thinking the world and its destiny from this side of the globe.

– 9 –

Thinking the World

When Sultan Badur wanted to go in the night to Portugal
or Brazil, or to Turkey or Arabia or Persia, all he had to
do was eat a little *bangua* (hashish).
Garcia da Orta, *Colóquios dos simples*,
'Colóquio Octavo' (1563)

What time is it there? Why be interested in lands and in
people living thousands of miles away? Turkish or American, the gaze at distant lands has appeared to us above all
as a gaze both domineering and concerned, as troubled
about the destiny of others as troubling in its engagements
and its expectations. But this gaze was also prompted by
another concern, less explicit but equally fundamental: the
desire to give some coherence to, and make sense of, a
representation of a world turned upside down by the
Iberian discoveries.[1] This is as true of Latin Christendom,
which had seen its intellectual foundations and religious
beliefs undermined, as of the Ottoman Empire, discon-
certed by the planetary advances of the Spanish and Portuguese. Since the beginning of the sixteenth century, in
different parts of the Catholic monarchy, geographers,
missionaries, government officials and members of the

local elites, some of European origin, some not, some of them adventurers, had come to realize that they were operating within a new, fluid and extendable reality, which was gradually spreading to encompass the whole of the terrestrial globe. Some of them even tried to think this unprecedented globality. Both inside Europe and outside it, they tried to define and to situate the space in which they lived, or in which they were interested, within this globality.

A New Image of the World

There were many ways open to them. On the European side, the most sensible was to opt for a pacific and Eurocentric point of view, in the manner of the *Theatre of the World*. The beautiful and proud Europe who adorns the frontispiece of Ortelius's atlas reigns over a planet without apparent conflicts. Cosmographical, geographical and cartographical, this 'Antwerp way' prepared for the advent of a triumphant modernity, that of a Northern and Atlantic Europe. Between Catholicism and Protestantism, as scientific as it could be in the sixteenth century, it breathed that reassuring familiarity which makes it still so close to us today. But other interpretations within Europe contested the right to impose their own image of the world. On the Catholic side, the *Relationi Universali* (or 'world reports') of the Piedmontese Giovanni Botero, a pupil of the Jesuits, was supported by vast quantities of information which offered a vision of the world imbued with the swaggering fervour of the Counter-Reformation.[2] For this ardent defender of Catholicism, one of the most lucid thinkers of his day, the Iberians had saved the planet. Without the conquests of the Portuguese and the Castilians, the Muslims 'would now be masters of the world'.[3] Botero was worried by how few Christians there were in the world, and very conscious of the political and military power of the Ottomans, strong right arm of Islam, as

Spain was of Roman Christendom.[4] This recognition, tinged with admiration, did not stop him from reviving the call for a crusade or from imagining a linguistic counter-offensive based on a systematic use of Arabic, which would denounce the errors of Islam and hold Mahometan practices up to derision.

Still on the Catholic side, but considerably less orthodox, the *Monarchy of Spain* of the Dominican Tommaso Campanella offered a messianic-millenarian interpretation of the destiny of the Crown of Spain. 'It is clear', he wrote, 'that he who will lay low the Turkish Empire will be master of the world.' Did the Turk not aspire to 'lordship of the world'? 'He calls himself universal lord like the king of Spain, who calls himself Catholic, that is, universal, so that they both vie for domination of the universe.'[5] Tommaso Campanella indicated two great spaces outside Europe which he saw as crucial,[6] the Ottoman Empire, to which he paid particular attention, and 'the other hemisphere, that is, the New World',[7] 'justly' dominated and possessed by Spain. It is with America, moreover, that Campanella ends his world tour.

On the Protestant side, Walter Ralegh's *History of the World* also made the opposition between Christianity and Islam an essential motor of future history.[8] Ralegh laid the foundations of English colonialism, Botero fought for a planetary Catholicism, Campanella reinvigorated Iberian imperialism by the prophecies of Scripture. All these Europeans, and many others with them, summoned up tools, interpretations and beliefs in order to respond to the challenges of an expanding world and to highlight the role of America.

Real or Virtual?

In what way are these preoccupations and dispositions of the late Renaissance of concern to us? Many people then imagined the destiny of the globe and of America on the

basis of a schematic vision of the world, biased but effective, which opposed Latin Christendom to the Ottoman
Empire and Islam. This Manichean schema continues, in
other forms, to condition our own imaginaries, so relent-
lessly is it churned out by the press, the cinema, television
and the Internet. As in the sixteenth century, the two
camps are in accord in each demonizing the other.[9]

In the sixteenth century this other was often a loathed
intruder, whether it be the Christian invader in Andalusia
or the Muslim merchant in the Indian Ocean.[10] The *moros/
cristianos* antagonism, so soon established in America and
imprinted on the minds of the Indians, was only one of
many versions of this dualist schema. In Mexico City, in
Istanbul and in Naples, the Ottoman Empire was seen as
playing a crucial role on the world chessboard. Seen from
Mexico or Naples, the threat was Turkish and Islamic, as
if Islam haunted Catholic horizons everywhere; whereas in
Istanbul the Anonymous Chronicler and his friends tried
to communicate the opposite idea through the strategies
of the Sublime Porte. In all these places, the future of the
globe was conceived as a ruthless confrontation between
the Iberian monarchy and the Ottoman Empire, or between
the religions they championed: 'Arms', wrote Campanella,
'can do nothing against religion: against it only another
religion which is better can succeed, even if it is without
arms, or what is worse, as long as it pleases the people or
its arms are superior.'[11]

Discourse and fears coexisted with a more pragmatic
and clear-sighted appreciation of where power lay on the
planet. What effect did this have in the diplomatic and
military spheres? The Christendom–Islam duality did not
prevent the king of France from making deals with the
Turks, or the English and Spanish from flirting with Persia,
or the Portuguese from negotiating with the Great Mughal,
or all of them from acknowledging the colossal power of
China.[12] It was as if the rejection of Islam or of the Christian West was constantly being superimposed on a rather
more complex geopolitics.

The victory of Lepanto led to outbreaks of rejoicing in the Christian part of the planet but was of little long-term benefit to Spain, even signalling the end of the great Mediterranean confrontations with the Turks.[13] Over and above the planetary appetites awakened by a period of globalization, the 'universal' sovereigns knew the limitations of their power, whether it be the sultan or the king of Spain.[14] By putting a damper on the calls for a crusade, the victory of Lepanto allowed Philip II to confront other enemies, much closer to home and more pressing: the England of the odious Elizabeth I, the Dutch of the rebel provinces, the stubborn France of the Huguenots. The supporters of a crusade were well aware that the European arena remained of paramount importance. Even Giovanni Botero acted as eulogist for a Catholic and Roman planet which seemed to be more concerned with Protestant rivals than with the Infidel. The Catholicization of the world had to confront the considerably more dangerous projects of the English and the Dutch, who cared little for the souls and salvation of the peoples to be colonized.

It was the same in the Protestant camp. Though not closing his eyes to the fact that Spain was the greatest power to have emerged in Europe since the fall of the Roman Empire, Ralegh still hoped that England, France and the Low Countries would find the means to get the better of it.[15] Having taken refuge in France, Campanella did a U-turn and changed sides. The man who had once lauded the new Spanish Cyprus and denounced the Turkish peril now backed the king of France against the Spanish monarchy and predicted a great reign for the future Louis XIV. At the dawn of the seventeenth century the time for a Hispano-Turkish confrontation had passed. It was not the last crusade that was brewing, but the Thirty Years War, which would tear Europe apart. It was the planetary rivalries between the European powers that would make battlefields and seas run with blood from Brazil to Angola and from the Indian Ocean to the coasts of Mexico. Though it did not disappear, the Turkish threat came to be concentrated in central Europe – the second siege of Vienna was in 1683. Elsewhere it remained a virtuality, regularly rating a mention and being denounced in the nostalgic writings which still called for a crusade against Islam.

So there remained the virtual scene in which two conceptions of the world confronted each other. It was in no way negligible. Islam was used in the construction of a dynamic vision of the planet that was developed in Spanish America, in Portuguese Asia and in Western Europe. It acted as foil for the virtues of Christianity as well as highlighting the rifts in a Christendom which would gain by taking the Ottoman threat more seriously in order to overcome its own divisions and unite against the 'impious sect'. This is surely the role of Islam in Giovanni Botero's *Relationi Universali*. Where did the New World fit in? For Botero the discovery of 'the other hemisphere' had been the wonder of the world, but it was the Christianization of America that was marking a major step towards the religious unification of the peoples of the earth, because it provided an exemplary model of Westernization. The New World represented, in this regard, the reverse of the worlds of Islam.

In all these scenarios, America, magnificent jewel in the crown of the Spanish Empire, loomed large in the eyes of observers: a land to be conquered for Sir Walter Ralegh[16] and the Anonymous Chronicler of Istanbul, a bastion to be reinforced for Heinrich Martin and Campanella; and for some already a promised land or continent of refuge. If the Turks triumphed, according to Campanella, empire and priesthood would pass to the New World and Europe would be ruined. It is interesting to find in his writings, a quarter of a century later, the ideas of the Dominican Francisco de la Cruz, who had defended to the death the thesis of a transfer of the leadership of the West across the Atlantic. The lands of Islam and America were two powerhouses of the imagination in a universe in the process of being globalized, and they each referred to the other, in

particular the Christians and sometimes in a remarkably
radical fashion.

The world consciousness which emerged in the sixteenth century was closely bound up with the propagat-
ion of the faith and religion, and not only because the
popes of the fifteenth century had played in anticipation
the role of notaries for Iberian globalization. In Istanbul,
in Lima and in Mexico City alike, religious concerns were
unquestionably one of the motors for the apprehension
of the world. The long-awaited fall of the Ottoman Empire,
the anticipated revenge on Islam in America and the crushing of the Old World by the Turks were symmetrical and
antithetic expressions of a monotheism with planetary
ambitions, greedy for conquests and thirsty for convers-
ions. The religions of the Book offered then, as they offer
today, an explanatory framework and universalist perspectives, and their efficiency should not be underestimated in
a period of globalization. The sense of belonging to a
common humanity, and of sharing a millennia-long history
that had begun with the Creation, encourages the emergence of interpretative models which lead to thinking the
world from the standpoint of an irredeemably reductive
universality; a world leading eventually to one same end:
'The end of the world is nigh, there will be only a single
flock (*unum ovile*) . . . then Christ will come for the judgement and that will be the end (*et sic finis*)'.[17]

The Mysteries of the Future

Real or virtual, in the sixteenth century the battle between
Christianity and Islam was read in the stars and in the
prophecies. The idea that astrology can help to think the
world makes us smile today, but it fascinated the men and
women of the Renaissance – Catholic and Protestant,
Christian and Muslim, Mexican and Chinese. In *The
Essence of History* the great Turkish historian Mustafâ
Alî of Gallipoli does not hesitate to describe the baleful

consequences for the Ottoman Empire of the great comet of 1577.[18] At this time, the heritage of the learning of Eastern, Greek and Roman Antiquity, brilliantly synthesized in the *Tetrabiblos* of Claudius Ptolemy, father of judicial astrology, constituted a Euro-Mediterranean patrimony which transcended confessional frontiers. Astrology was then a 'science', recognized as such, and one able regularly to reinvent itself. Very few people were yet bold enough to deny the value of astrological predictions. It needed a Giordano Bruno to dare to attack astrology, demolish its Aristotelian foundations and proclaim the infinity of the universe, and he was burned at the stake. Rome would eventually put its house in order. In condemning judicial astrology, the bull of 5 January 1586 marked a significant shift in the attitude of the Church. But the new post-Tridentine line was slow to win acceptance in Christendom and it did not prevent a Heinrich Martin from being interested in the political consequences of planetary conjunctions or from publishing his conclusions with the backing of the colonial authorities. Nor, thousands of miles away, in the prisons of the Inquisition, did it prevent Tommaso Campanella from being as concerned as our German about the impact of the 'great conjunction' of Jupiter and Saturn, in the sign of the fire of Sagittarius, on 24 December 1603.[19] Same sky, same source: Campanella used the predictions of the astrologer Antonio Torquato a few years before Heinrich Martin did the same. Like many Europeans, they were both aware that, in his *De eversione Europae prognosticon* (1480), the physician of Ferrara had predicted the conversion of the Turks.[20] That 'the empire of the Moon' – the Turkish empire – was doomed to collapse was believed as firmly in Naples as it was in Mexico City.

Astrology brought with it a stream of prophecies and predictions, often attached to sacred texts. Implicit in Heinrich Martin, exploited in depth by Campanella, the eschatological capital did more than respond to the challenges then being posed by the beginnings of the unification of the globe. Its very existence reveals the links that united the Christian and Muslim imaginaries, often through the intermediary of the Jewish milieus who moved freely between the two. This common thread underlay all sorts of affective reactions and intellectual constructions. Messianisms and millenarianisms, everywhere bolstered by astrological speculations and fuelled by the great upheavals of the sixteenth century, constituted a collective patrimony which brought ways of thinking, hoping and fearing closer together. The prophecies circulated from one society to the other; it hardly matters that they changed their meaning and direction, they were always there, ready to be made use of, that is, ready for new exegeses. Beyond the divisions between peoples and religions, and in spite of everything in them that seems to us archaic and irrational, they, too, played their part in the emergence of a world consciousness. It was not by chance that one of the major centres of publication for prophetic literature was Venice. The presses of the Lagoon made as great a contribution to knowledge of the globe as to the interpretation of its ultimate purpose, combining the most scrupulous observation and the wildest speculation, without contemporaries seeing any contradiction.

The triumph of modernity and globalization notwithstanding, astrology and prophecies are far from having disappeared from our planet. The Lady is stubborn, not only because she is still the only one who can unveil the future, but also because she seems to transcend times and cultures. The contemporary proliferation of horoscopes, mages and soothsayers means astrology cannot be dismissed as a body of bygone knowledge. The taste for occultism, the world-wide craze for *The Da Vinci Code* and its epigones and the proliferation of websites attest to the survival, not to say rude health, of this type of knowledge at a time of accelerated globalization. A Google search for the word horoscopes in April 2008 gave more than 56 million hits.[21] There can be no doubt that Heinrich Martin – or his alter ego – would have had no difficulty today in finding publishers or readers for his manual and his predictions, even if he was obliged to water down his 'incorrect' remarks about the Turks. The aplomb with which Martin puts forward his prognoses and dramatizes his speculations has lost none of its appeal. In any case, since they have found sites to accommodate them, the prophecies of Nostradamus (4.5 million hits) and Joachim de Fiore have probably never had as many readers and followers. Is it any surprise that the Web is home to innumerable speculations about the future of the world, the fate of Islam, the triumph of empires and the end of time?

As we have seen, it was Franciscan and Dominican millenarianism that went furthest in exploring the relationship between America and Islam. Faced with the advance of the Turks, scourge of God and of Europe, the New World presented itself as a land of refuge, bringing hope to an elect humanity and the promise of salvation for the Christo-European heritage. The Franciscan Motolinía, like the Dominican Francisco de la Cruz, cultivated this hope. Others followed suit in the seventeenth century and, even in the Age of Enlightenment, the *Orbe novo seráfico* of the Franciscan Jaboatão resurrected this trend by celebrating the role of a Brazil guided by the order of St Francis.[22] America has not ceased to be a land of purity facing an Old World in decline, or Islam to be seen as a satanic spectre. Nor have the messianisms crossed with millenarianisms of Mexico and Peru abandoned our world, where every project for universal domination tends to revive this ancient heritage. They are found on the Islamic side as much as round the White House or among the voices that support Israel in the hope of one day reuniting all Christians in a Jerusalem purged of its Muslim occupants. It is hardly surprising that, from such a perspective, the war against Iraq could be interpreted as fulfilling one of the prophecies of the Apocalypse, or that global warming has become an indisputable and universal sign of the approach of the end of the world. In the face of a Catholicism at bay, some Protestant Churches, some strands within Islam and some Asiatic sects have become breeding grounds for eschatological beliefs and expectations, which often take disturbing forms. Paradoxically, behind the innocence of the entertainment and the box office records, the mass cinema also plays a large role in disseminating this heritage. The Hollywood studios, by bringing these fears to the screen, regularly reactivate them all over the planet. The *Star Wars* series, the *Matrix* trilogy and *Terminators 1, 2* and *3* impose their procession of messianic leaders and apocalypses with the aid of Dolby sound and special effects. The old schemas are endlessly recycled, 'reloaded' to quote *Matrix*, before being globalized. To think the world is a mammoth task which has fostered, and continues to foster, all sorts of fundamentalisms, so huge is the challenge. The hunt for the Beast which Heinrich Martin invited us to join has long been under way.[23]

A View of the World

The writings of Heinrich Martin and the Anonymous Chronicler of Istanbul do not simply alert us to the strong links existing between the great monotheistic religions and numerous esoteric trends and our own way of seeing or foreseeing the world. In simultaneously encompassing the different parts of the planet, they each in their own way give an account of the diversity of the societies and the regions of the globe as well as of the ties that now united them. The Europeans and many other peoples with them discovered that, for better or worse, it was becoming difficult to manage without others.[24] These two texts were part of a common trajectory constructed by societies born of the Ancient world, Christianity and Islam, that is, of a long period during which these societies had taken turns at getting to know and extending their control over the spaces that surrounded them. Western Europeans may, in the thirteenth century, have tried to make a first breakthrough to the world by knocking at the gates of Mongol

Asia, but Arab historians and geographers had preceded
them by hundreds of years in the discovery of the globe.[25]
In the fifteenth century, thanks to the discoveries of
the Portuguese and the Castilians, Christian knowledge
received a formidable boost, enormously enhanced by the
tardy recovery of the heritage of Ancient geography. Power
and the desire to know seemed then to be inextricably
linked. If Spain had received its universal mission, explained
Campanella, it was because it had experienced the desire
to know the world, *perché desiderò di conoscerlo*. 'To
know the world is already half way to possessing
it . . . Columbus felt the desire to know the world, which
is the son of God.'[26]

During the course of the sixteenth century cartographers and cosmographers developed increasingly accurate and well-researched tools. From this point on, large
quantities of oral information, manuscripts, printed material and maps spread throughout Europe, America and the
rest of the planet. The Ottoman world was not isolated
from this development, even if it seemed more oriented
towards the Muslim Mediterranean and Asia. Global
thinking would have been impossible without this cosmo-
graphic, geographic and proto-ethnographic labour. Of
course, it was not all immediately exploited or assimilated.
How, indeed, were these oceans of information to be organized, when they were constantly being added to, as shown
by the maps that were corrected, completed and even
redrawn year after year? Is this not the very same obstacle
we ourselves encounter, on a daily basis, for want of something with which to impose order on the ceaseless flow of
information about the world? There remains the breadth
of the horizons of Heinrich Martin and the Anonymous
Chronicler. In both of them there shines through an intellectual and spiritual conviction that it was now impossible
to ignore the rest of the world. Their gaze soars above the
spaces of the globe in their anxiety to push back horizons
as far as was possible. Heinrich Martin claimed to be able
to predict eclipses in places to which no one had ever been,

in countries that might be uninhabited, even uninhabit-able. The Anonymous Chronicler devoted page after page to descriptions of lands that no Muslim had ever visited. In each case, we sense the tentative and confused emerg-ence of a global conception of the world, which found expression in intellectual constructions that always took a singular form.

As I reach the end of this book, I would like to have compared these different testimonies even more closely. It is only by taking account of their contemporaneousness and by assessing their similarities and differences that one can come close to a reading of the world that is neither systematically European nor exclusively Christian. Beyond the religious and political biases specific to each text, their common quest for a global vision brings these voices strangely close to our own twenty-first century. The histor-ian will be encouraged by them to envisage what a history released from its ancestral reflexes and its national strait-jacket might be. Neither Heinrich Martin nor the Anony-mous Chronicler thought in the national contexts within which modernity has confined us. Neither needed to dis-engage from the ways of addressing the past and space put in place in the nineteenth century, and which have now become inadequate, not to say obsolete, in the face of the upheavals affecting our planet. Even more crucial, in neither Mexico City nor Istanbul could the global be con-fused with the European or the Atlantic; no Europe without Islam or America . . . This is perhaps one of the lessons to be learned from these texts which engage in a constant dialogue with the Old World without lapsing into Eurocentrism.

Conclusion
What Time is it There?

'What time is it there?' This is surely also, and perhaps primarily, a personal matter, one of those private questionings without which we might well lack the inclination to spend so much time in dusty archives.

Both the Anonymous Chronicler and Heinrich Martin expended far more energy in examining other worlds than was necessary to fill the pages of their manuscripts. I would like to have been able to dig deeper into what these two intellectual undertakings conceal. What did America represent in the imaginary of the Anonymous Chronicler or Heinrich Martin? How important was Europe in their eyes? The answers are all the more difficult to find in that both these men constantly camouflage their feelings. What memories were really evoked for Heinrich Martin by his native city, the heretical and chilly Hamburg where he had been born and to which he returned at the end of his adolescence, visiting its Lutheran churches? What did Catholic Spain, which cast its dark shadow over the *Repertory*, mean to him? If we add Mexico City and New Spain to the mental baggage of our German, we have at least three worlds coexisting in the secrecy of his thoughts. Strange accusations were levelled against him late in his Mexican career. Torrential rains had fallen in the region and he had not wished to see swept away by the flood the colossal tunnel he had dug to drain the Valley of Mexico; he had preferred, it was said, to see the city disappear under the waters, as if, before dying, our Dr Faust had settled his score with the 'heart of New Spain'. The city remained flooded for many years. As for the Anonymous Chronicler, what game was he playing when he concealed his identity while at the same time sticking stubbornly to his aim of producing a pioneering work? Why this fixation on the New World, why this nostalgia for Andalusia? And why this opacity, made worse by the gaps in our own knowledge of the Turkish and Muslim world?

The texts I have briefly examined reveal only the tip of the iceberg, since our authors had to avoid criticisms that might have cost them dear. The porosity that is revealed, in spite of everything, between Seville and Hamburg, between the Ottoman Empire and the Christian world and between Spanish Mexico and the indigenous societies hints at the strength of the secret ties which crossed political and religious frontiers. By the sixteenth century, like Heinrich Martin and Miguel de Cervantes, thousands of individuals had passed from one world to the other, voluntarily or not, crossing the Mediterranean, the Atlantic, the Pacific or the Indian Ocean. They had all suffered the teething troubles of a modernity that has become ours and that is everywhere revealed as made up of compromises and cross-fertilizations that were constantly being renegotiated.[1]

Societies were for a long time mistrustful of these sorts of mobility. The Spaniards from America who returned to the Peninsula remained *Indianos* and never became Europeans again. For the Japanese authorities, the Christianized Japanese and mestizos who had settled outside the archipelago were persona non grata. It was not in the best interests of the Jews of Spain who had taken refuge in the Ottoman Empire or of the renegades to set foot in the Peninsula again. They had all learned to live between several worlds. Between total rootlessness and substitute ethnocentrisms there was space for many accommodations, acknowledged or, more often, disguised. It is surely no coincidence that the Renaissance writer who is most 'alive' to us today is Miguel de Cervantes, who spent five years in Algiers, at the heart of that African Babel, and who never stopped writing about the Muslim worlds as if, up to a point and in his own way, he was part of them.[2]

To pass from one world to the other, in either direction, was an ordeal and an initiation in every sense of the word. It remains so today, even though we have access to many ways of reducing the distance and the time. Paradoxically, this technical advantage further heightens the contrast we feel between a dizzying sense of proximity and an uncontrollable impression of compartmentalization and fragmentation. It is this that is explored by a film full of forebodings, Alejandro González Iñárritu's *Babel* (2006). From the Moroccan desert to the dusty roads of Mexico and the United States, by way of the Japan of post-modern metropolises, the camera of González Iñárritu reveals the invisible thread which connects human beings wherever they are on the planet. It achieves today the feat that was mocked by the canon in *Don Quixote*, a 'comedy' which successively unfolds in Europe, Asia, Africa and America, 'in the four quarters of the globe'. *Babel* plays on the singularity of each locale the better to link the whole, as if contemporary cross-fertilizations ought to prepare us to slither or zigzag from one world to the other, and no longer only mix them. This is what the Taiwanese hero of *What Time is it There?* was trying to do when he struggled to catch hold of a universe he had never entered; what González Iñárritu achieved by filming Japan and Morocco with as much skill as he filmed Mexico. One can belong to many worlds and at many times without seeking to reduce them or standardize them. Perhaps this is our only way of getting to grips with the globality that surrounds and overruns us?

Notes

Introduction

1. Publisher's note: Throughout this book, the word *mondialisation* is translated as 'globalization', although Gruzinski uses these words to refer to two distinct phenomena. *Mondialisation* refers to the worldwide diffusion of economic, political, religious and cultural features and their mixing with local ones, whereas 'globalization', for Gruzinski, refers only to the capacity of certain components of European civilization to spread all over the world, imposing standards and patterns without any mixing or interference with local realities, differences and traditions: see Serge Gruzinski, *Les Quatre Parties du monde* (Paris: La Martinière, 2004). The same word in English, 'globalization', refers to what are, for Gruzinski, two connected but distinct worldwide processes.

1 Istanbul/Mexico City: The Eye of the Sages

1. Thomas D. Goodrich, *The Ottoman Turks and the New World. A Study of Tarih-i Hind-i garbi and Sixteenth Century Ottoman America* (Wiesbaden: Otto Harrassowitz, 1990), p. 74. My discussion here is based on this translation.
2. Robert Mantran (ed.) *Histoire de l'Empire ottoman* (Paris: Fayard, 1989), pp. 156–7; Daniel Goffman, *The Ottoman Empire and Early Modern Europe* (Cambridge: Cambridge University Press, 2002), pp. 137–88.

3. 'Clime' meaning the space on the mappa mundi and the geographical maps lying between two circles (latitudes) parallel to the equator.

4. Goodrich, *Ottoman Turks*, p. 19.

5. For its author, see Goodrich, *Ottoman Turks*, p. 19. The anonymous Turk indicates that he has given his work the title *Hadis-i nev* ('*Fresh News*'): ibid., p. 75.

6. Alexandra Merle, *Le Miroir ottoman. Une image politique des hommes dans la littérature géographique espagnole et française (XVIe–XVIIe siècle)* (Paris: Presses de l'Université de Paris-Sorbonne, 2003), p. 100, quoting the French traveller Philippe Du Fresne-Canaye, who discovered the city in 1573.

7. Diogo do Couto, *Diogo do Couto e a década 8a da Asia*, ed. Maria Augusta Lima Cruz, Comissão Nacional para as Comemorações dos Descobrimentos (Lisbon: Imprensa Nacional, 1994), pp. 205–7; Gian Carlo Casale, 'The Ottoman Age of Exploration: Spices, Maps and Conquest in the Sixteenth Century Indian Ocean', unpublished Ph. D. thesis, Harvard University, 2004; Gian Carlo Casale, 'A Caliph, a Canal and Twenty Thousand Cannibals: Global Politics in the 1580s', pp. 10–11 (*www.usc.edu/schools/ college/crcc/private/ierc/Caliph_Canal_Cannibals.pdf*); Gian Carlo Casale, '"His Majesty's Servant Lutfi": The career of a previously unknown sixteenth-century Ottoman envoy to Sumatra, based on an account of his travels from the Topkapi Palace archives', *Turcica. Revue d'études turques*, 37 (2005), pp. 43–81.

8. Naimur Rahman Farooqi, *Mughal-Ottoman Relations: a Study of Political and Diplomatic Relations Between Mughal India and the Ottoman Empire, 1556–1749* (Delhi: Idarah-i Adabiyat-i Delli, 1989), p. 17.

9. A milieu which included Emir Mehmed bin Emîr Hasan es-Sudi, who, though he did not write the *Tarih-i Hind-i garbi*, corrected the copy intended for the sultan. His brother, Seyid Ebu Mehmed Mustafa, was the author of a universal history.

10. Henrico Martínez, *Repertorio de los tiempos* (Mexico: Secretaría de Educación Pública, 1958), p. 258. For the Jewish diaspora from Spain into the Ottoman Empire, see Jonathan I. Israel, *Diasporas Within a Diaspora, Jews,*

Crypto-Jews and the World Maritime Empires (1540–1740) (Leiden: Brill, 2002), pp. 41–96; Henry Méchoulan, *Les Juifs d'Espagne, histoire d'une diaspora, 1492–1992* (Paris: Liana Lévi, 1992), and especially Gilles Veinstein, 'L'Empire ottoman depuis 1492 jusqu'à la fin du XIXe siècle', pp. 361–87.

11. Bernard Lewis, *Islam and the West* (Oxford: Oxford University Press, 1993), pp. 77–8.

12. Merle, *Le Miroir ottoman*; and for Spain, the classic work of Albert Mas, *Les Turcs dans la littérature espagnole du siècle d'or: recherches sur l'évolution d'un thème littéraire*, 2 vols (Paris: Centre de recherches hispaniques, 1967).

13. Goodrich, *Ottoman Turks*, pp. 9–16. We should note in particular the world map of the Ottoman admiral Piri Reis (1513) and his treatise on the Mediterranean and the New World, *Kitab-i bahriye* (*Book of maritime lore*), which dates from 1521.

14. Goodrich, *Ottoman Turks*, pp. 236–8, 240–6, 61.

15. Ibid., p. 366.

16. Some of the miniatures do not correspond to the text, such as the audience granted by Ferdinand the Catholic to Christopher Columbus (no. 2 in the Bayezit ms.).

17. Martínez, *Repertorio*, pp. 224, 229.

18. Nicolás Rangel, *Historia del toreo en México* (Mexico: Editorial Cosmos, 1980), p. 34; Max Harris, *Aztecs, Moors and Christians. Festivals of Reconquest in Mexico and Spain* (Austin: University of Texas Press, 2000), pp. 150–1.

19. Françisco de la Maza, *Enrico Martínez, cosmografo e impresor de Nueva España* (Mexico: Secretaría de Educación Pública, 1943; Universidad nacional autónoma de México, 1991) (references are to the 1991 edn). He was born between 1554 and 1560, according to Willard F. King, *Juan Ruiz de Alarcón, letrado y dramaturgo. Su mundo mexicano y español* (Mexico: El Colegio de México, 1989), p. 76; Valerie R. Mathes, 'Enrico Martínez of New Spain', *Americas*, 33, 1 (July 1976), pp. 62–77; Luisa Schell Hoberman, 'Enrico Martínez, printer and engineer', in David Sweet and Gary Nash (eds), *Struggle and Survival* (Berkeley: University of California Press, 1981), pp. 331–46.

20. Maza, *Enrico Martínez*, p. 18.

21. Arriving in Poland in 1579, the Florentine Fausto Sozzini, also known by the name of Socinus (1539–1604), founded a Church whose spiritual and intellectual influence spread widely from Rakow; see Emile G. Léonard, *Histoire générale du protestantisme* (Paris: Presse Universitaire de France, 1961), vol. 2, p. 47.

22. Heinrich Martin makes one reference to Poland in his universal chronology, for the year 1573: 'En este mismo año por orden de Selim, emperador de Turcos, entró en el reino de Polonia grandísimo ejército de Tártaros, talando y robando le tierra, y vinieron a batalla campal con los Polacos, en la cual fueron los Tártaros vencidos y muertos 40,000 de ellos, que fue notable pérdida para el Turco': Martínez, *Repertorio*, p. 266.

23. Michael J. Mikos, 'Monarchs and magnates: maps of Poland in the sixteenth and eighteenth centuries', in David Buisseret (ed.), *Monarchs, Ministers and Maps. The Emergence of Cartography as a Tool of Government in Early Modern Europe* (Chicago–London: University of Chicago Press, 1992), pp. 170–1.

24. A land of lakes and marshes, Courland is bounded to the north-east by the Dvina, which separates it from Livonia, adjoins eastern Prussia in the south, has the Gulf of Riga as its northern border and is in the west bathed by the Baltic Sea.

25. The history of the printed book in Riga began in the 1580s. In 1582 the papal legate, the Jesuit Antonio Possevino, embarked on the spiritual reconquest of the Baltic countries and asked Rome to send him a copy of the Catholic catechism of Canisius. A German priest translated it into Latvian and 1000 copies were printed in 1585. There was a rapid counter-attack in the form of the publication, in 1586, of a translation of Luther's Small Catechism. In 1588, a true printing house opened under the direction of a Dutchman, Nicolaus Mollyn, at the invitation of the Council of the city of Riga. Four years later, Mollyn published an *Astrological prognosis*, a genre which would later become a speciality of Heinrich Martin in Mexico. See Nicholas Viksnins, 'The early history of Latvian books', *Lituanus, Lithuanian Quarterly Journal of Arts and Sciences*, 19, 3 (Fall 1973) (*http://lituanus.org/1973/73_3_O2.htm*).

26. Once in Mexico, Heinrich Martin would hardly have failed to refer to any past collaboration with the Society of Jesus.
27. Martínez, *Repertorio*, p. 121. Should this population with Asiatic features be identified with the Livs or Livonians? A year later, in Spain, Gregorio García repeated this information in his treatise *Origen de los Indios del Nuevo Mundo* (Valencia: Pedro Patrico Mey, 1607).
28. Son of the second viceroy of New Spain, Luis de Velasco held this post until 1595 and then again from 1607–11, before being appointed head of the Council of the Indies.
29. The printer's mark used by Heinrich Martin was a swan, an emblem which adorned the works of the Seville printer Montes de Oca and a Madrid printer Guillermo Drouy, in business until 1589. Heinrich Martin must already about now have bought Drouy's stock with the idea of reselling it in Mexico, or perhaps using it himself. There were four printing houses operating in Mexico at the beginning of the seventeenth century: Melchor de Ocharte, Pedro Balli, Diego López Davalos and Heinrich Martin (Maza, *Enrico Martínez*, p. 14). Heinrich Martin began by making characters for Adrianus Cornelius Cesar, who was planning to open a printing house in Cuautitlan, in the vicinity of Mexico. The first book he published, in 1599, was a text in Nahuatl: *Compendio de las excelencias de la Bulla de la Santa Cruzada en lengua mexicana compuesto por el padre Fray Elias de San Juan.* This was the last book published in Mexico in the sixteenth century, and it ended the series known as the Mexican Incunabula.
30. For the scientific and technical milieu in Mexico, see María Luisa Rodríguez-Sala, *Letrados y técnicos de los siglos XVI y XVII* (Mexico: Universidad nacional autónoma de México & Miguel Angel Porrúa, 2002).
31. AGN (Mexico), *Inquisición*, Real fisco, vol. 29, fol. 269r/v.
32. Francisco Fernández del Castillo, *Libros y libreros en el siglo XVI* (Mexico: Fondo de cultura económica, 1982), pp. 522–32.
33. He published invitations to defences of theses, and he tackled linguistic questions by publishing the *Discurso de la antigüedad de la lingua cantabra*, a defence of the Basque language written by the painter Baltasar de Echave Orio

(1607), and a guide to conversation in Spanish and Nahuatl compiled by Pedro de Arenas (1611).

34. *Poeticarum Institutionum Liber . . . collectore eiusdem Societatis sacerdote qui eidem presidet congregationi Antonio Rubio praefecto* (Mexico: Heinrich Martin, 1605); Martínez, *Repertorio*, p. XXXVII.

35. Martin had planned to explain to his readers how agriculture should be adapted to the '*temperamento y clima de esta Nueva España*'. The other treatise, on the *fisionomia de rostros*, was intended to reflect on the meaning that should be accorded to the facial features and behaviour of the child: Martínez, *Repertorio*, pp. 270–1.

36. *El semejante a sí mismo*, quoted in Maza, *Enrico Martínez*, pp. 114–15, 117.

37. Jean Delumeau, *La Civilisation de la Renaissance* (Paris: Arthaud, 1967), p. 293; Robert Mantran, *Histoire d'Istanbul* (Paris: Fayard, 1996).

38. Francisco López de Gómara was the author of a *Historia general de las Indias*, the second part of which is the *Historia de la conquista de México* [1552]; 13 Spanish editions are known between 1552 and 1555, 15 in Italian between 1556 and 1576, 9 in French between 1568 and 1588 and 2 in English between 1578 and 1596. In 1526, Gonzalo Fernández de Oviedo published in Toledo his *Sumario*, or *De la natural hystoria de las Indias*; this work ran to four editions in Italian between 1534 and 1565. Peter Martyr d'Anghiera was the author of the *Decades*, which were among the first works to make known to Europeans the discovery of America by Columbus and the conquest of Mexico by Cortés. To Agustín de Zarate we owe the *Historia del descubrimiento y conquista del Peru*, the first edition of which dates to 1555; French, Dutch, English and Italian versions followed.

39. Goodrich, *Ottoman Turks*, pp. 74–5. For how Asiatics saw or did not see Europe in the sixteenth and seventeenth centuries, see Sanjay Subrahmanyam, 'Taking stock of the Franks: South Asian views of Europeans and Europe 1500–1800', *The Indian Economic and Social History Review* (New Delhi), 42, 1 (2005), pp. 69–100.

40. Apart from the English versions of C. Adler and Thomas D. Goodrich, the work was partially translated into French in

the eighteenth century and into Italian in the nineteenth century: Goodrich, *Ottoman Turks*, p. 30.

41. By the Secretaría de Educación Pública in 1958, in facsimile by Condumex in 1981 and in 1991 by Consejo nacional para las artes.

42. Lewis, *Islam and the West*, p. 79.

43. Texts circulated from America to Asia and from Asia to America *via* Italy, thanks to the Italian translations of the great chronicles of the New World in the case of the *Tarih-i Hind-i garbi*, and to the histories compiled in the Peninsula in the case of the *Repertory*. Thomas D. Goodrich has been able to identify several of the translators used by the Ottoman author: Alfonso Ulloa for Agustín de Zarate, Agostino de Cravaliz and Lucio Mauro for the *Historia* of López de Gómara: Goodrich, *Ottoman Turks*, pp. 34–5.

44. Sergeï Eisenstein, *The Film Sense*, trans. Jay Leyda (New York: Harcourt Brace Jovanovich, 1942), p. 19.

2 'What Time is it There?'

1. Giovanni Battista Ramusio, 'Tommaso Giunti alli lettori', *Navigationi et Viaggi*, I (Venice: Tommaso Giunti, 1563).

2. José de Acosta, *The Natural and Moral History of the Indies* (Durham, NC–London: Duke University Press, 2002), p. 26.

3. Jorge Manuel dos Santos Alves, *O domínio do norte de Samatra. A história dos sultanatos de Samudera-Pacém e de Achém, e das suas relações com os Portugueses (1500– 1580)* (Lisbon: Sociedade histórica da Independência de Portugal, 1999), p. 168.

4. Thomas D. Goodrich, *The Ottoman Turks and the New World. A Study of Tarih-i Hind-i garbi and Sixteenth Century Ottoman America* (Wiesbaden: Otto Harrassowitz, 1990), pp. 183, 408.

5. Antônio Galvão, *Tratado dos descobrimentos* [Lisbon: 1563] (Barcelos: Livraria Civilização Editoria, 1987), p. 51.

6. Goodrich, *Ottoman Turks*, pp. 206–9, 195 n. 572.

7. Ibid., p. 100.

8. Serge Gruzinski, *Les Quatre Parties du monde. Histoire d'une mondialisation* (Paris: La Martinière, 2004); Serge Gruzinski, *Histoire de Mexico* (Paris: Fayard, 1996).

9. Bernardo de Balbuena, *La grandeza mexicana y compendio apologético en alabanza de la poesía*, ed. Luis Adolfo Domínguez (Mexico: Editorial Porrúa, 1990), p. 122.

10. Goodrich, *Ottoman Turks*, p.100; Balbuena, *La grandeza mexicana*, pp. 77–8.

11. On the Portuguese case, see Luis Felipe F. Tomaz and Jorge Santos Alves, 'Da cruzada ao quinto império', *A Memoria da nação* (Lisbon: Sá da Costa Editoria, 1991), pp. 81–165.

12. Joan-Pau Rubiés, *Travel and Ethnology in the Renaissance: South India Through European Eyes, 1250–1625* (Cambridge: Cambridge University Press, 2000).

13. Francisco López de Gómara, *La Historia de las Indias y conquista de México* (Zaragoza: Agustín Millán), fol. III.

14. 'Desejoso de ver mundo': Galvão, *Tratado dos descobrimentos*, p. 142; 'os que mais provincias & terras viram por suas livres vontades': ibid., p. 142.

15. For Antiquity, one thinks of the impulse given by the conquests of Alexander: see Federica Cordano, *La geografia degli antichi* (Bari: Laterza, 2006), p. 102. For the Mongols, Peter Jackson, *The Mongols and the West, 1221–1410* (London: Pearson Longman, 2005).

16. Ruy González de Clavijo, *Embajada a Tamerlán*, ed. Francisco López Estrada (Madrid: Editorial Castalia, 2004).

17. *Conquista de las Indias de Persia e Arabia* (Salamanca: 1512), by Martín Fernández de Figueroa, a Spaniard from Salamanca who had taken part in the Portuguese expeditions to Asia.

18. Acosta, *Natural and Moral History of the Indies*, p. 53.

19. This was the *Instrucción nautica para el buen uso y regimiento de las Naos* of Diego García de Palacio (Mexico: Pedro Ocharte, 1587); see José Toribio Medina, *La Imprenta en México (1539–1821)* (Mexico: Universidad nacional autónoma de México, 1989), vol. 1, p. 281.

20. Ramusio, 'Discourse on spices', *Navigationi et viaggi*, I (Venice: 1550).

21. Goodrich, *Ottoman Turks*, pp. 144–5.

22. Alexandra Merle, *Le Miroir ottoman. Une image politique des hommes dans la littérature géographique espagnole et française (XVIe–XVIIe siècle)* (Paris: Presses de l'Université

de Paris-Sorbonne, 2003), p. 39; Geoffroy Atkinson, *Les Nouveaux Horizons de la Renaissance française* (Paris: Droz, 1935).

23. Francisco de Vitoria, *Relectio de Indis. La questione degli Indios*, ed. A. Lamacchia (Bari: Levante Editori, 1996); Francisco de Vitoria, *De jure belli*, ed. Carlo Galli (Bari: Laterza, 2005); Paulo Suess (ed.), *A conquista espiritual da América espanhola. 200 documentos, século XVI* (Petropolis: Vozes, 1992), p. 510.

24. J. Llaguno, *La Personalidad jurídica del indio y el II Concilio Provincial Mexicano* [1585] (Mexico: Porrúa, 1963), pp. 183–4.

25. Suess, *A conquista espiritual*, pp. 506, 510.

26. José de Acosta, *De procuranda indorum salute*, 1. I, ch. 1 (Madrid: Centro superior de investigaciones científicas, 1984), vol. 1, p. 76.

27. Suess, *A conquista espiritual*, p. 225.

28. Peter Sloterdijk, *Esferas II. Globos. Macrosferologia* (Madrid: Siruela, 2004), p. 829.

29. Gregorio García, *Origen de los Indios del Nuevo Mundo* [1607] (Mexico: Fondo de cultura económica, 1981).

30. The Iberian Peninsula was the first European region to benefit from a cartographic coverage worthy of the name, but this was not at the expense of the listing of the overseas possessions: Geoffrey Parker, 'Maps and ministers: the Spanish Habsburgs', in David Buisseret (ed.), *Monarchs, Ministers and Maps. The Emergence of Cartography as a Tool of Government in Early Modern Europe* (Chicago–London: University of Chicago Press, 1992), pp. 124–42.

31. Geoffrey Parker, 'David or Goliath? Philip II and his World in the 1580s', in Geoffrey Parker and Richard L. Kagan (eds), *Spain, Europe and the Atlantic World. Essays in Honour of John H. Elliott* (Cambridge: Cambridge University Press, 1995), p. 246.

32. Hernán Cortés, *Cartas y documentos*, ed. Mario Hernández Sánchez-Barba (Mexico: Porrúa, 1963), p. 508.

33. Ramusio, 'Discourse on spices', *Navigationi et viaggi*.

34. Parker, 'David or Goliath?', pp. 247–8.

35. José de Acosta, 'Parecer sobre la guerra de la China, México, 15 de marzo de 1587', *Obras completas* (Madrid: Biblioteca de autores españoles, 1954), p. 331.

36. 'Los Españoles tienen derecho natural para peregrinar y contratar en todas las naciones extrañas del mundo, y quien les veda este trato y entrada les hace injuria': ibid., p. 332.
37. Diogo do Couto, *O soldado prático*, ed. Reis Brasil (Lisbon: Publicações Europa-América, 1988).
38. Goodrich, *Ottoman Turks*, p. 143.
39. Alonsa de la Mota y Escobar, *Descripción geográfica de los reinos de Nueva Galicia, Nueva León y Nueva Viscaya* (Mexico: Pedro Robredo, 1940), p. 102.
40. Balbuena, *La grandeza mexicana*, pp. 79, 78.
41. Sanjay Subrahmanyam, 'On world historians in the sixteenth century', *Representations*, 91 (2005), p. 28.
42. Serge Gruzinski, *La Pensée métisse* (Paris: Fayard, 1999), trans. as *The Mestizo Mind: the Intellectual Dynamics of Colonization and Globalization* (New York–London: Routledge, 2002).
43. Suess, *A conquista espiritual*, p. 501; José de Acosta, *De procuranda Indorum salute*, *Obras completas* (Madrid: Atlas, Biblioteca de autores españoles, 1954), p. 450.
44. Subrahmanyam, 'On world historians in the sixteenth century', p. 39.
45. Though this tends to be contradicted by the evidence collected for Persian visitors to India: Muzaffar Alam and Sanjay Subrahmanyam, *Indo-Persian Travels in the Age of Discoveries, 1400–1800* (Cambridge: Cambridge University Press, 2007).
46. Duarte de Sande, *Diálogo sobre a missão dos embaixadores japoneses à cúria romana* [1590], ed. Américo da Costa Ramalho (Macao: Fundação Oriente, 1997).
47. Carmen Bernard, *Un Inca platonicien, Garcilaso de la Vega* (Paris: Fayard, 2006).
48. Ebba Koch, *Mughal Art and Imperial Ideology. Collected Essays* (Oxford: Oxford University Press, 2001), pp. 51, 57.
49. Acosta, *Natural and Moral History of the Indies*, p. 17.
50. François Hartog, in his introduction to Polybe, *Histoire* (Paris: Gallimard, 2003), p. 19.
51. Hartog is interested in the way the Greek historian envisaged the history of the world as a 'general' or global history, more than as a universal history: 'Polybius ultimately gives a spatial, geographical turn to his history, shifting from the

general (*to katholou*) to the catholic (*historia katholikê*)':
ibid., pp. 20–23.

52. Rodrigo de Vivero employs the notion of *mapa general*, in
his *Du Japon et du bon gouvernement de l'Espagne et des
Indes*, ed. Juliette Montbeig (Paris: SEVPEN, 1972).

3 The International of the Cosmographers

1. J. M. Rogers, '"The Gorgeous East": trade and tribute in
the Islamic empires', in Jay A. Levenson (ed.), *Circa 1492:
Art in the Age of Exploration* (Washington–New Haven–
London: National Gallery of Art–Yale University Press,
1991), pp. 69–74; Jerry Brotton, *Trading Territories.
Mapping the Early Modern World* (London: Reaktion
Books, 1997), p. 99.

2. Thomas D. Goodrich, *The Ottoman Turks and the New
World. A Study of Tarih-i Hind-i garbi and Sixteenth
Century Ottoman America* (Wiesbaden: Otto Harrassowitz,
1990), pp. 73, 75.

3. Marco A. Moreno Corral, 'La astronomía en el México del
siglo XVIIe', *Ciencias*, 54 (April–June 1999), pp. 52–9.

4. María Luisa Rodríguez-Sala, *El eclipse de luna. Misión
científica de Felipe II en Nueva España* (Huelva: Biblioteca
Montaniana, Universidad de Huelva, 1998).

5. Born in Linz, Georg von Peurbach (1423–61) taught astronomy and mathematics. Master of Regiomontanus, he prepared the ground for the upholders of the heliocentric
system.

6. Moreno Corral, 'La astronomía en el México del siglo
XVIIe', p. 59.

7. See Bernabé Navarro, 'La *Physica speculatio* de fray Alonso
de la Veracruz y la filosofía de la naturaleza o Cosmovisión
Aristotélica en el Nuevo Mundo', in Mauricio Beuchot
and Bernabé Navarro (eds), *Dos homenajes: Alonso de la
Veracruz y Francisco Xavier Clavigero* (Mexico: Instituto
de Investigaciones Filosófiacas, Cuadernos 57, Universidad
nacional autónoma de México, 1992), pp. 13–24; Armando
Barranón, 'Copernico en la física de Alonso de la Veracruz',
Razón y palabra (August–September 2004) (razóny palabra.
org.mx).

8. Juan Díez Freile, *Sumario compendioso de las quentas de plata* (Mexico: 1556). For the question of the growth of the sciences in the New World, see Jorge Cañizares-Esguerra, *Nature, Empire and Nation. Explorations of the History of Science in the Iberian World* (Stanford: Stanford University Press, 2006).

9. 'Rasguño de las provincias de la Nueva México', in Valerie R. Mathes, 'Enrico Martínez of New Spain', *Americas*, 33, 1 (July 1976), pp. 62–77; 'Mapa de Nuevo México por el cosmógrafo Enrico Martínez' [1600], Archivo General de Indias, Patronato 1-1, legajo 3/22, ramo 12.

10. Heinrich Martin was also the author of a report 'Sobre las ventajas que podrían traer el descubrimiento, conquista y pacificación de las Californias' (Archivo General de Indias, Mexico, 372). See also 'Derrotero desde Acapulco al Cabo Mendocino por Gerónimo Martin Palacios con los diseños de la costa hechos por Enrico Martínez, 8 y 19 de Noviembre 1603' (Real Academia de la Historia, M. 23), also 'Treinta y dos mapas o croquis de la costa y puertos descubiertos por Sebastian Vizcaino desde el Puerto de Navidad hasta el cabo Mendocino' (Archivo General de Indias, Gobierno, Audiencia de México, Legajo 372).

11. Goodrich, *Ottoman Turks*, p. 77.

12. Henrico Martínez, *Repertorio de los tiempos* (Mexico: Secretaría de Educación Pública, 1958), p. 5.

13. Goodrich, *Ottoman Turks*, p. 79.

14. The Anonymous Chronicler contrasted the prosperous Northern hemisphere to a Southern hemisphere still 'unknown and veiled or . . . entirely submerged by sea water': ibid., p. 82. See Gottfried Hagen, *Ein osmanischer Geograph bei der Arbeit. Entstehung und Gedankenwelt von Katib Celebis Gihannüma, Studien zur Sprache, Geschichte und Kultur der Türkvölker*, ed. György Hazaiz (Berlin: Klaus Schwarz Verlag, 2003), especially ch. 2, pp. 79–120.

15. Goodrich, *Ottoman Turks*, pp. 80, 86.

16. Ibid., p.137. This scholarship was collected in the *Sûrya Siddhânta*, an astronomical treatise written in India around 400. The Anonymous Chronicler associated with it the works of Aryabhatta, an Indian mathematician and astronomer (476–550), and the *Almagest*.

17. Born in Baghdad, al-Masûdi travelled to Spain, India and China, spending the last years of his life in Syria and Egypt.

18. Nasir al-Din al-Tusi (1201–74), Persian astronomer and doctor, was one of the founders of trigonometry. His work greatly influenced that of Copernicus. Ibn al-Wardi was the author of the *Pearl of Wonders and the Uniqueness of Things*.

19. Goodrich, *Ottoman Turks*, pp. 110–11.

20. Ibid., pp. 143–4.

21. A native of Cordoba, Khashkhash Ibn Saîd Aswad set off from Delba (Palos) and reached a unknown land ('ard marjûla') from which he returned with fabulous treasures. Al-Masûdi's map of the world shows this zone in the 'ocean of darkness and fog'.

22. Idrîsî, *La Première Géographie de l'Occident*, ed. François Bresc and Annliese Neff (Paris: GF-Flammarion, 1989).

23. Goodrich, *Ottoman Turks*, pp. 118–20, 146. The anonymous author notes the possibility that the American continent extended into the northern hemisphere as far as China.

24. Ibid., pp. 74, 153, 157.

25. Ibid., p. 141.

26. Ptolemy gave eight. See Numa Broc, *La geografia del Rinascimento, Cosmografi, geografi, viaggiatori, 1420–1620* (Modena: Panini Franco Cosimo, 1996), p. 9.

27. Goodrich, *Ottoman Turks*, pp. 90–2, 101.

28. *Voyageurs arabes, Ibn Fadlan, Ibn Jubayr, Ibn Battuta*, Collection 'Bibliothèque de La Pléiade' (Paris: Gallimard, 1995), p. 12.

29. Goodrich, *Ottoman Turks*, p. 115.

30. Ibid., pp. 151–2. His description of this part of the world led the author to call for *djihad* and refer to the exploits of 'a brave man named Tarik' who had seized Andalusia with only 700 men.

31. Ibid., p. 95.

32. *Book of maritime lore*: ibid., p. 11.

33. L. Bonelli, 'Del Muhît, o "Descrizione dei mari delle Indie" dell'Ammiraglio turco Sìdì Afi detto Kiâtib-i-Rûm', *Rediconti della Reale Academia dei Lincei* (1894), pp. 751–77.

34. It is a copy of a large Gastaldi map of 1560: Goodrich, *Ottoman Turks*, p. 14, n. 24.

35. Georg Schurhammer, 'Una ipotesi sulla fine di Antonio Pigafetta', *Gesammelte Studien: Orientalia*, ed. László Szilas (Rome: 1963), pp. 455–61.
36. Goodrich, *Ottoman Turks*, pp. 146, 302.
37. Paul Binding, *Imagined Corners: Exploring the World's First Atlas* (London: Headlines Books, 2003), p. 245.
38. Martínez, *Repertorio*, p. 119.
39. As if his experience in Courland had taken him to the borders of a Europe which excluded the Grand Duchy.
40. These subdivisions are probably taken from the *Theatrum* of Abraham Ortelius.
41. Martínez, *Repertorio*, p. 119.
42. The Strait took its name from the Chinese province of Ania, mentioned in an edition of 1559 of the work of Marco Polo. In 1592 the navigator of Greek origin, Juan de Fuca, claimed to have sailed from the Pacific to the North Sea.

4 Antwerp, Daughter of Alexandria

1. Numa Broc, *La geografia del Rinascimento, Cosmografi, geografi, viaggiatori, 1420–1620* (Modena: Panini Franco Cosimo, 1996), p. 5; Francesco Prontera, *Geografia e geografi nel mondo antico* (Bari: Laterza, 1990).
2. To which we should add Johannes de Sacroboso, author of *The Sphere*, a summary of the astronomical and cosmographical knowledge of Antiquity, of which 144 Latin editions are known: Broc, *La geografia del Rinascimento*, p. 12.
3. Francisco de la, Maza, *Enrico Martínez, cosmografo e impresor de Nueva España* (Mexico: Secretaría de Educación Pública, 1943), p. 118; Thomas D. Goodrich, *The Ottoman Turks and the New World. A Study of Tarih-i Hind-i garbi and Sixteenth Century Ottoman America* (Wiesbaden: Otto Harrassowitz, 1990), p. 80.
4. Ptolemy was interested in the size of the Earth, proposed two types of conical projection and pondered the best way of drawing a map of the world.
5. The eight books of Ptolemy's *Geography* describe an *oikumene* oriented west–east, occupying almost half the northern part of the sphere.
6. When Ptolemy reduced the length of the circumference calculated by Eratosthenes and believed that the emerged lands

were more extensive than the seas and the oceans, he was wrong on both counts, but these errors were probably inspired by the continuing increase in Roman power, an earthly power of unprecedented extent.

7. Goodrich, *Ottoman Turks*, pp. 80, 83, 85: 'It is a strange circumstance and an unusual affair that one section of the people full of calamity would exert itself so strongly in this way and would go from west to east and put up with the adversities of the wind and the trials of the seas.'

8. Ibid., p. 110.

9. This Nestorian Christian from the Lower Euphrates learned Greek and translated some hundred works. His son translated Euclid.

10. See Arnaldo Momigliano, 'Polybius' reappearance in Western Europe', in *Essays in Ancient and Modern Historiography* (London: Blackwell, 1977), pp. 79–98; Polybe, *Histoire* (Paris: Gallimard, 2003).

11. At Vicenza (?1475), then at Bologna and Rome (1478). For an overall view, see Broc, *La geografia del Rinascimento*.

12. Binding, *Imagined Corners*, p. 183.

13. For the question of the relationship to the Ancients and the role of Antiquity in the birth of modernity, see Louise Bénat Tachot, 'L'Antiquité: obstacle ou auxiliaire pour la découverte du Nouveau Monde', in Louise Bénat Tachot and Serge Gruzinski (eds), *Passeurs culturels. Mécanismes de métissage* (Presses universitaires de Marne-la-Vallée, Editions de la Maison des sciences de l'homme), pp. 219–38.

14. Binding, *Imagined Corners*, p. 194.

15. Broc, *La geografia del Rinascimento*, p. 8.

16. The first Latin edition ran to 325 copies. The Dutch version was published the year after with the title *Theatre oft Toonneel des Aerdtbodems*. The French version, the *Théâtre de l'univers*, came out in 1572: Binding, *Imagined Corners*, p. 254.

17. The letter of Gerardus Mercator which accompanied new editions of the *Theatrum* was lavish in its praise of the convenience of an object so easily accessible, that took up so little space and could even be 'carried about wherever we please': Binding, *Imagined Corners*, p. 225.

18. Jerry Brotton, *Trading Territories. Mapping the Early Modern World* (London: Reaktion Books, 1997), pp. 176, 123.

19. Giorgio Mangani, *La Signification providentielle du* 'Theatrum Orbis Terriarum' (Brussels–Antwerp: 1998); Giorgio Mangani, 'Abraham Ortelius and the hermetic meaning of the cordiform project', *Imago Mundi*, 50 (1998), pp. 59–83.

20. Binding, *Imagined Corners*, pp. 202–3, 253.

21. Brotton, *Trading Territories*, p. 175, quoting Hessels, *Ortelii epistolae*, 86.

22. Ibid., p. 171. Christopher Marlow described his play *Tamburlaine* as a great game of chess: kings and conquerors were the pieces and the 'theatre' of Ortelius the chessboard.

23. In this sense, the *Theatrum* was one of the great intellectual enterprises of the Catholic monarchy. The production of the *Theatrum* cannot be dissociated from the publication of the polyglot Bible on the presses of the printing house of Christopher Plantin, favoured printer of the Spanish sovereign. If the atlas established the image of the world of 'the King's Geographer', the Bible of 'the King's Printer' offered the Philippian version of the Holy Scriptures. The two 'tools' had a universal ambition; each in its own way founded a world view.

24. The *Theatrum* took on a clearly anti-Spanish tone in an abbreviated verse version, the *Spieghel der Wereld* (*Mirror of the World*), produced by the Antwerp poet Peeter Heyns, still deeply affected by the sack of Antwerp by the brutal Spanish soldiery. The Dutch version of the *Theatre of the World* became the mirror of Spanish cruelty. Its America reflected past or future atrocities in the Low Countries; see Benjamin Schmidt, *Beyond Innocence. The Dutch Imagination and the New World, 1570–1670* (Cambridge: Cambridge University Press, 2001), p. 72.

25. Ibid., p. 129. See the engraving *America* of Jan Van der Straet, produced in Antwerp, in a series entitled *Nova reperta*. The association of America and cannibalism was a theme that persisted throughout the sixteenth century and its inclusion among the elements considered typically 'American' further distanced the European reader from the realities of colonial America.

26. Binding, *Imagined Corners*, p. 252. The maps are accompanied by texts on the back because geography was the eye of the historian: ibid., p. 223.

27. Martin Heidegger, *Chemins qui ne mènent nulle part* (Paris: Gallimard, 2006), p. 123, English trans. *Pathmarks*, ed. William McNeill (Cambridge: Cambridge University Press, 1998).

28. The atlas nevertheless contains a map of the New Spain added in 1579: Howard F. Cline, 'The Ortelius Map of New Spain 1579 and related contemporary materials, 1560–1610', *Imago Mundi*, 16 (1961), pp. 98–115. In 1584 three new maps of America were added to that of Mexico, one of which was of Peru, *Peruvia auriferae regionis tipus*. See also R. W. Shirley, *The Mapping of the World. Early Printed World Maps 1472–1700*, The Holland Press, Cartographia Series, vol. 9 (London: Holland Press, 1983).

29. Henrico Martínez, *Repertorio de los tiempos* (Mexico: Secretaría de Educación Pública, 1958), p. XLV.

30. Ibid., p. 162; Abraham Ortelius, *Teatro de la tierra universal* (Antwerp: Plantin, 1588).

31. Martínez, *Repertorio*, pp. 162, 165. Pegasus became the emblem of the Creoles of Mexico.

32. Ibid., pp. 169, 192, 195.

33. Ibid., p. 98.

34. Rodrigo de Vivero, *Du Japon et du bon gouvernement de l'Espagne et des Indes*, ed. Juliette Montbeig (Paris: SEVPEN, 1972), pp. 49, 74.

35. Juan de Torquemada, *Monarquía indiana* [1615], 7 vols (Mexico: Universidad nacional autónoma de México, 1975–83).

36. Luiz Felipe de Alencastro, *O trato dos viventes. Formação do Brasil no Atlántico Sul* (São Paulo: Companhia das Letras, 2000).

37. Henri Lancelot Voisin de La Popelinière, *Les Trois mondes*, ed. Anne-Marie Baulieu (Geneva: Droz, 1997).

38. Idrîsî, *La Première Géographie de l'Occident*, ed. François Bresc and Annliese Neff (Paris: GF-Flammarion, 1989), p. 52.

39. Seyyidi 'Ali Reis, *The Travels and Adventures of the Turkish Admiral Sidi Ali Reïs in India, Afghanistan, Central Asia and Persia During the Years 1553–1556* (London: 1899).

5 Histories of the World and of the New World

1. Thomas D. Goodrich, *The Ottoman Turks and the New World. A Study of Tarih-i Hind-i garbi and Sixteenth Century Ottoman America* (Wiesbaden: Otto Harrassowitz, 1990), p. 351.

2. Benjamin Schmidt, *Beyond Innocence. The Dutch Imagination and the New World, 1570–1670* (Cambridge: Cambridge University Press, 2001), pp. 69–70, 95.

3. The author of the *Decades* and *De Orbe novo* (1516), Pietro Martire d'Anghiera was read in the version of three first decades given by Giovanni Battista Ramusio (*Navigationi et Viaggi*, Venice, 1556 or 1565). Gonzalo Fernández de Oviedo, who published *De la natural historia de las Indias* in 1526, was used in one of the Italian editions of this work (they appeared between 1534 and 1565) and in the compilation of Ramusio (*Navigationi et Viaggi*). Francisco López de Gómara was the author of *Historia de las Indias* (1552) which ran to some fifteen editions in Italian between 1556 and 1576. It was the translations of Agostino de Cravaliz and Lucio Mauro which were used by the Anonymous Chronicler of Istanbul. Lastly, the *Historia del descubrimiento y conquista del Peru* (1555) of Agustín de Zarate, in the translation of Alfonso Ulloa (1563), provided precious information on the Peru of the conquistadors.

4. One of the manuscripts of the *Tarih-i Hind-i garbi* has marginal annotations which translate the table of contents of the third volume of Ramusio.

5. Benjamin Arbel, 'Maps of the world for Ottoman princes? Further evidence and questions concerning "The Mappamondo of Hajji Ahmed"', *Imago Mundi*, 54 (2002), pp. 19–29.

6. Goodrich, *Ottoman Turks*, pp. 14 n. 21, 15, 19.

7. Ibid., p. 30.

8. Ibid., pp. 19, 305–36.

9. The *Rhetorica christiana* of Diego Valades, which deals with the evangelization and the missions, came out in Perugia in Latin in 1579. For the pre-Hispanic societies, most of the information available also circulated in manu-

script form; the major writings of the Franciscans Motolinía and Sahagún and of the Dominican Durán, to quote only the most famous, were published only in the nineteenth century.

10. Goodrich, *Ottoman Turks*, pp. 176, 257.
11. Ibid., pp. 176, 257, 259, 264.
12. This part contains the account of the voyage of Magellan.
13. Unless, on the model of the Hindus of the Mughal Empire, they had received the status of *dhimmi*, as suggested to me by Gilles Veinstein.
14. Alexandra Merle, *Le Miroir ottoman. Une image politique des hommes dans la littérature géographique espagnole et française (XVIe–XVIIe siècle)* (Paris: Presses de l'Université de Paris-Sorbonne, 2003); Encarnación Sanchez García et al. (eds), *España y el Oriente islámico entre los siglos XV y XVI* (Istanbul: Editorial Isis, 2007).
15. Henrico Martínez, *Repertorio de los tiempos* (Mexico: Secretaría de Educación Pública, 1958), p. 231.
16. Ibid., p. 172. The same idea is found in Giovanni Botero, *Relationi universali* (Brescia: 1599), part 1, p. 196.
17. Martínez, *Repertorio*, p. 230. Bâyezîd I ruled from 1389 to 1402.
18. See the play devoted to Tamburlaine (Tamerlaine) and Bajazet (Bâyezîd I) by Christopher Marlowe, which inspired the libretto of an opera by Vivaldi in the eighteenth century.
19. Francesco Sansovino, *Historia Universale dell'Origine, Guerre et Imperio de Turchi* (Venice: 1564); see Luigia Zilli, 'Francesco Sansovino compilatore della Historia universale de Turchi', *L'Europa e il Levante nel Cinquecento. Cose turchesche* (Padua: Unipress, 2001), pp. 49–63; Stéphane Yerasimos, 'De la collection de voyage à l'Histoire universelle. La *Historia Universale de Turchi* de Francesco Sansovino', *Turcica*, 22 (1988), pp. 19–41.
20. Constantino Ponce de la Fuente (1502–60) and Agustín de Cazalla (1510–59) had been chaplains to Charles V.
21. Martínez, *Repertorio*, p. 251.
22. Antonio de Herrera y Tordesillas, *Historia de lo sucedido en Escocia* (Madrid: Pedro Madrigal, 1589).
23. Martínez, *Repertorio*, p. 257.
24. Ibid., p. 258.

25. The dates and events recorded by Heinrich Martin are: 1522: capture of Rhodes by the Turks; 1535: capture of La Goulette by Charles V; 1541: defeat of the fleet of Charles V before Algiers; 1560: defeat of the Spanish at Djerba (Gelves) at the hands of the Turks; 1563: siege of Oran and Mazalquivir (Mers el-Kebîr); 1564: capture of Peñón de Vélez by the Spanish; 1565: siege of Malta by the Turks; 1571: capture of Cyprus by the Turks and victory of Lepanto; 1574: capture of La Goulette and Tunis by the Turks; 1578: defeat of Sebastian of Portugal at Kasr al-Kebîr.

26. Martínez, *Repertorio*, p. 266.

27. He reminded his readers of the defeat of Louis of Hungary at Mohacs (1526), the siege of Vienna (attributed to 1531 instead of 1529), an attack by the 'Tartars' on Poland (1573 – in fact in 1574 and 1575) and the victories of 'the king of Persia' against the Turks in 1578 and 1585.

28. Martínez, *Repertorio*, p. 257.

29. Ibid., pp. 257, 122–3.

30. Goodrich, *Ottoman Turks*, pp. 115, 151.

31. Martínez, *Repertorio*, p. 42.

32. Antonio de Herrera y Tordesillas, *Historia general de los hechos de los Castellanos en las islas i tierra firme del mar oceano*, 7 vols (Madrid: Emprenta Real, 1601–15).

6 The History of the World is Written in the Stars

1. Thomas D. Goodrich, *The Ottoman Turks and the New World. A Study of Tarih-i Hind-i garbi and Sixteenth Century Ottoman America* (Wiesbaden: Otto Harrassowitz, 1990), p. 253.

2. Henrico Martínez, *Repertorio de los tiempos* (Mexico: Secretaría de Educación Pública, 1958), p. 232. In the fifteenth century Georgius of Hungaria had already referred to 'the sect of the Turks' as 'bloody Beast': Georgius of Hungaria, *Des turcs: traité sur les moeurs, les coutumes et la perfidie des Turcs*, trans. and ed. Joel Schnapp (Toulouse: Anacharsis, 2007), p. 48. Contemporary with Heinrich Martin, voices as respectable as that of Tommaso Campanella were calling for the destruction of the Turks: 'Let us unite for the ruin of such

a great wolf which has torn two empires and two hundred kingdoms from us by force and by art, exploiting our discords'. Educated Europeans repeated these imprecations up to the end of the seventeenth century, including Gerónimo Monterde, who published in 1684 a *Juicio según letras humanas y divinas de la destrucción del imperio otomano y Agareno, y recuperación de los santos lugares*.

3. Goodrich, *Ottoman Turks*, pp. 115–16.

4. Martínez, *Repertorio*, p. 232.

5. Ibid., p. XXXIX.

6. Carlos Alberto González Sánchez, *Los mundos del libro. Medios de difusión de la cultura occidental en las Indias del los siglos XVI y XVII* (Seville: University of Seville, 2001), pp. 214, 223. In Peru the indigenous chronicler Guaman Poma de Ayala took his inspiration from the 'repertories' of Andrés de Li and Andrés de Zamorano. See Victoria Cox, *Guaman Poma de Ayala entre los conceptos andino y europeo del tiempo* (Cuzco: Centro Bartolomé de Las Casas, 2002).

7. Antonio de Morga, *Sucesos de las islas Filipinas* [Mexico: 1609] (Madrid: Polífemo, 1997), p. 154.

8. See Alfredo López Austin, 'Un repertorio de los tiempos en idioma náhuatl', *Anales de Antropología*, X (1973), pp. 285–96; David Eduardo Tavarés, 'Social reproduction of late postclassic ritual practices in early colonial central Mexico. A seventeenth-century Nahua devotional miscellany: Fonds mexicain 381', Famsi, Foundation for the Advancement of Mesoamerican Studies, Inc. (*http://www.famsi.org/reports/96039/section03.htm*).

9. *Instrucción nauthica par el buen uso y regimientos de los naos, su traça y govierno conforme a la altura de* México (Mexico: Pedro Ocharte, 1587), in José Toribio Medina, *La Imprenta en México (1539–1821)* (Mexico: Universidad nacional autónoma de México, 1989), vol. 1, p. 280; Elias Trabulse, *Historia de la ciencia en México* (Mexico: Fondo de cultura económica, 1984), vol. 2, p. 17.

10. Martínez, *Repertorio*, pp. 42–96. Like all *lunarios*, that of Heinrich Martin contained 'las conjunciones, cuartos y oposiciones del sol y luna . . . las cuales se han regulado con la puntualidad a mí posible para el meridiano de esta ciudad de México': ibid., p. 41.

11. In 1607 Juan de Barrios discussed the relationships between medicine and astrology in his *Verdadera cirugía médica y astrología* (Mexico: Fernando Balli, 1607).
12. Martínez, *Repertorio*, pp. 218, 224, 219.
13. The sources of the astrologer of Mexico were legion, and not particularly original. I will quote only Johannes de Sacroboso and his publisher Francesco Giuntini (1523–90), Carmelite and theologian, whose *Speculum* developed a defence and illustration of astrology which borrowed freely from the astronomical tables of Copernicus; the German Johannes Müller von Konigsberg (1436–76) alias Regiomontano, mathematician, pupil of Georg Peurbach, author of logarithmic tables, and in particular of a calendar printed in Venice in 1476; and the cardinal Pierre d'Ailly (1351–1420), author of a great geographical encyclopaedia, the *Imago mundi* (c. 1410). The *Repertorio* mentions another figure of European renown, Lucas Gauricus or Luca Gaurico (1476–1558), a Neapolitan, author of a *Tratatus astrologicus* (Venice: 1552). Martin was clearly very familiar with one of the great names of Spanish science, Pedro Ciruelo (1470–1548), author of an *Apostelemata astrologiae christianae* (1521), and had read Valentin Nabod, author of a work of reference on astrology, *Enarratio elementorum astrologiae* (Cologne: 1560), based on the work of Alcabicius.
14. Geoffrey Parker, *The World is not Enough. The Grand Strategy of Philip II* (New Haven: Yale University Press, 1998).
15. Miguel Angel de Bulnes, *La Imagen de los musulmanes y del norte de Africa en la España de los siglos XVI y XVII: los carácteres de una hostilidad* (Madrid: Centro superior de investigaciones científicas, 1989), pp. 75–6.
16. AGN (Mexico), Inquisición, vol. 328, exp. 30, fols 131r–133v.
17. What Heinrich Martin called the 'congregaciones del pueblo mahometano'.
18. Serge Gruzinski, *L'Aigle et la Sibylle. Fresques indiennes des couvents du Mexique* (Paris: Imprimerie nationale, 1992).
19. Heinrich Martin does not tell us – or did not know – that he had nevertheless been elevated to the patriarchate by Mehmed II in 1454, soon after the fall of Constantinople.

See A. Pertusi, *Fine di Bisanzio e fine del mondo. Significato e ruolo storico delle profezie sulla caduta di Costantinopoli in Oriente e Occidente*, ed. E. Morini (Rome: Istituto Storico per il Medio Evo, 1988); Stephane Yerasimos, *La Fondation de Constantinople et de Sainte-Sophie dans les traditions turques* (Istanbul-Paris: Iletisim Yayinlari, 1990).

20. In the Spanish edition of 1558, or that of 1602; a first edition in Latin of the *Theatrum Orbis Terrarum* (Antwerp: Gielis Coppens Van Diest), had been available since 1570. This first modern atlas ran to forty editions in the sixteenth century.

21. Martínez, *Repertorio*, p. 225.

22. For astrologers and astrology in the sixteenth century, see Anthony Grafton, *Cardano's Cosmos: the World and Works of a Renaissance Astrologer* (Cambridge, Mass.: Harvard University Press, 2000).

23. Antonio Arquato or Torquato (Torquatus) had sent this prediction in 1481 to the king of Hungary Mathias Corvin. He had also predicted the coming of Luther and the sack of Rome; see D. Cantimori, *Eretici italiani del Cinquecento* (Turin: Einaudi, 2002); Eugenio Garin, *La cultura filosofica del Rinascimento italiano. Ricerche e documenti* (Florence: Sansoni, 1961; Milan: Bompiani, 2001).

24. Martínez, *Repertorio*, p. 226.

25. Ibid.

26. The dream of Murâd III evokes that of Nebuchadnezzar, who dreamed of a statue broken by a stone and a huge tree which 'reached unto heaven' (Daniel, 2, 3).

27. In the seventeenth century the Jesuit António Vieira invoked the Islamic tradition among the sources and the themes of his prophesies: 'Portugal há-de ser império quinto e universal, como se prova com a fé dos históricos, com o juízo dos políticos, com o discurso dos matemáticos, com as profecias dos santos, com as tradições dos mesmos maometanos, para cuja prova se têm feito e escrito doutíssimos tratados': *Obras inéditas*, II (Lisbon: J. M. C. Seabra and T. Q. Antunes, 1856–7), p. 87.

28. Martínez, *Repertorio*, p. 163.

29. Ibid., pp. 132–3.

30. In fact in 1087.

31. Martínez, *Repertorio*, pp. 134–5.

32. Ibid., p. 135.
33. Ibid., p. 139.
34. José de Acosta, *The Natural and Moral History of the Indies* (Durham, NC–London: Duke University Press, 2002), pp. 431–2.
35. Prudencio de Sandoval, *Historia de la vida y hechos del emperador Carlos V máximo, fortísmo, Rey Católico de España y de las Indias, Islas y Tierra firme del mar Océano*, 3 vols, ed. Carlos Seco Serrano (Madrid: Atlas, 1955–6 (Biblioteca de autores españoles, 80–2). Bishop of Tui and Pamplona, Sandoval (1553–1620) had only recently published his work (1604–6). Heinrich Martin quotes Book 2 (pp. 136–7).
36. For the Italian context, see Ottavia Niccoli, *Profeti e popolo nell'Italia del Rinascimento* (Bari: Laterza, 2007), pp. 89–121 (trans. Lydia G. Cochrane as *Prophecy and People in Renaissance Italy* (Princeton: Princeton University Press, 1990).
37. Martínez, *Repertorio*, p. 138.
38. Ibid., p. 139.
39. Bernardino de Escalante, *Discurso de la Navegación que los Portugueses hazen a los reinos y provincias de Orient* (Seville: 1577), p. 63.
40. Martínez, *Repertorio*, pp. 41, 104.
41. Ibid., p. 132.
42. Ibid., p. 134.

7 Islam at the Heart of the Monarchy

1. Including worries about purity and fear of contamination. See Andrew Wheatcroft, *Infidels. A History of the Conflict between Christendom and Islam* (London: Viking, 2003), p. 102ff.
2. Ramón Alba, *Acerca de algunas particularidades de las comunidades de Castilla* (Madrid: Editorial Nacional, 1975), p. 199.
3. Thomas D. Goodrich, *The Ottoman Turks and the New World. A Study of Tarih-i Hind-i garbi and Sixteenth Century Ottoman America* (Wiesbaden: Otto Harrassowitz, 1990), p. 152.

4. Wheatcroft, *Infidels*, p. 99.

5. Leopoldo Torres Balbas, *Algunos aspectos del mudejarismo urbano medieval* (Madrid: Real Academia de la Historia, 1954); Carmen Bernis, 'Modas moriscas en la sociedad cristiana española del siglo XV y principios del XVI', *Boletín de la Real Academia de la Historia*, CXLIV, 2 (1959), pp. 199–228; Cynthia Robinson, 'Mudejar revisited. A prolegoména to the reconstruction of perception, devotion and experience at the Mudéjar convent of Clarisas, Tordesillas, Spain (fourteenth century A.D.),' *Res*, 43 (Spring, 2003), pp. 51–77; Jerrilynn D. Dodds, Thomas F. Glick and Vivian B. Man (eds), *Convivencia: Jews, Muslims and Christians in Medieval Spain* (New York: G. Braziller, 1992).

6. Pinharanda Gomes, *A história da filosofia portuguesa*, vol. 3: *A filosofia arabigo-portuguesa* (Lisbon: Guimarães Editores, 1991), p. 271.

7. Festivals like the *mouriscas*, a Christianized and 'folklorized' heritage, would live on.

8. Antonio Garrido Aranda, *Moriscos e Indios* (Mexico: Universidad nacional autónoma de México, 1980), p. 36.

9. Gomes (*A filosofia arabigo-portuguesa*, p. 273) refers to two censuses of Moriscos in Portugal in 1603 and 1618. In 1612 Damião da Fonseca published in Rome his *Justa expulsión de los moriscos de España*, dedicated to Francisco de Castro, Spanish ambassador to Rome.

10. Gomes, *A filosofia arabigo-portuguesa*, p. 190.

11. The trajectory of certain words throws light on the transition from one civilization to another: the Latin word *sublimatum* gave the Arabic *sulaimâni*, which provided the Portuguese *solimão*.

12. Gomes, *A filosofia arabigo-portuguesa*, p. 293.

13. Ibid., p. 294.

14. João de Barros drew on Muslim sources in writing his *Décadas*: ibid., p. 280.

15. Alain de Libera, *Penser au Moyen Age* (Paris: Seuil, 1989), pp. 98–142.

16. Gomes, *A filosofia arabigo-portuguesa*, p. 286.

17. With a few exceptions such as the archbishop of Braganza, Teotónio of Braganza, who collected Arabic works. Some humanists like Clenardo vainly advocated the study of Arabic and Hebrew. The translation of the *Tarigh* (Antwerp,

1610) by Pedro Teixeira remained an exception and it was into Castilian: *Relaciones del origen, descendencia y succession de los reyes de Persia* . . .: Gomes, *A filosofia arabigo-portuguesa*, p. 281.

18. Ibid., p. 282.
19. L. P. Harvey, *Muslims in Spain, 1500 to 1614* (Chicago–London: Chicago University Press, 2005), pp. 122–203.
20. The Bull *Inter caetera* (4 May 1493) clearly established this sequence. See Paulo Suess, *A conquista espiritual da América espanhola* (Petropolis: Vozes, 1992), p. 249. Defeated at Granada, Islam held on to the African coasts of the western Mediterranean. Which explains why, in 1494, Fernando de Zafra suggested seizing Melilla, terminus for the caravans bringing gold from the Sudan. Portugal shared this unease and these enthusiasms. Cardinal Cisneros had asked Manuel for his support for his projected crusade. For Portugal no capture of Granada, but victory of Ceuta, in 1415: the shift from reconquest to conquest was as swift as in Spain but much earlier. The advance along the coasts of Africa was constantly coming up against black Islamized populations before new Muslim interlocutors appeared on the Asiatic horizon. When Manuel proclaimed himself king of *Além-Mar em Africa, senhor da Guiné e da Conquista, Navegação, Comércio de Etiópia, Arábia, Pérsia e India*, his title was more a programme of conquest than a list of territories actually under Portuguese control. The Portuguese victories at Azamor – Azemmour, on Cap Blanc – was met with popular enthusiasm. In his *Exhortação da guerra* the writer Gil Vicente presents Hannibal, the hero of the Punic Wars, announcing to the Christians that Africa would be seized from the Muslims, while Achilles asks the clergy to sell their goods to finance the crusade.
21. Psalm 19, 5 (In omnem terram exivit sonus eorum, et in fines orbis terrae verba eorum); Luis Felipe F. Tomaz and Jorge Santos Alves, 'Da cruzada ao quinto império', *A Memoria da nação* (Lisbon: Sá da Costa Editoria, 1991), pp. 81–165, at p. 128, n. 148.
22. Isaiah 65,17,18 (Et vidi caelum novum et terram novam . . .).
23. Alain Milhou, *Colomb et le messianisme hispanique* (Gap: Presses universitaires de la Méditerranée, 2007), pp. 385, 392; John Leddy Phelan, *The Millenial Kingdom of the*

Franciscans in the New World (Berkeley: University of California Press, 1970), p. 37; Alain Milhou, 'De la destruction de l'Espagne à la destruction des Indes: histoire sacrée et combats idéologiques', *Etudes sur l'impact culturel du Nouveau Monde*, vol. 3, pp. 11–54 (Paris: L'Harmattan, 1983); Abbas Hamdani, 'Columbus and the recovery of Jerusalem', *Journal of the American Oriental Society*, 99, 1 (January–March 1979), pp. 39–48.

24. The idea that he who would rebuild Jerusalem would come from Spain was taken from Joachim de Fiore and his interpreters: Phelan, *The Millenial Kingdom of the Franciscans*. p. 39. Columbus got his quotations from Joachim de Fiore from the work of Pedro de Aliaco, *De concordia astronomice veritatis cum theologia et cum hystoria narratione*; see Juan Gil, *Mitos y utopías del descubrimiento. I. Colón y su tiempo* (Madrid: Alianza Universidad, 1989), pp. 195–217.

25. Alain Milhou, 'La tentación joaquinita en los principios de la Compañía de Jesús. El caso de Francisco Borja y Andrés de Oviedo', *Florensia, Bollettino del Centro Internazionale di Studi Gioachimiti*, year VIII–IX (1994–5), pp. 193–239, at p. 194.

26. Joseph Pérez, *Isabelle et Ferdinand, rois catholiques d'Espagne* (Paris: Fayard, 1988), p. 310.

27. Marcel Bataillon, *Erasmo y España, Estudios sobre la historia espiritual del siglo XVI* (Mexico: Fondo de cultura económica, 1982), pp. 55–6.

28. Paolo Giovio, *Commentarii delle cose de Turchi* (Venice: Figliuoli di Aldo, 1531); Luís Vives, *De conditione vitae christianorum sub Turca* (Bruges: 1526); Luís Vives, *De Europae dissidiis et bello turcico dialogus* (Bruges: 1527).

29. Pérez, *Isabelle et Ferdinand*, pp. 310–11.

30. Lucette Valensi, *Fables de la mémoire. La bataille des trois rois* (Paris: Seuil, 1992).

31. Milhou, *Colomb et le messianisme hispanique*, p. 387.

32. Bartolomé de Las Casas, *Apologética historia sumaria*, vol. 2 (Mexico: Universidad nacional autónoma de México, 1967), p. 650; Bartolomé de Las Casas, *Obras*, vol. 110 (Madrid: Biblioteca de autores españoles, 1954), p. 111b, in *Octavo remedio*, written in 1542 and published in 1552; Alain Milhou, 'De la destruction de l'Espagne à la

destruction des Indes: histoire sacrée et combats idéologiques',
Etudes sur l'impact culturel du Nouveau Monde, vol. 1,
p. 30.

33. 'Según que ello mismos lo pronuncian por sus escrituras y
doctores', in ibid., p. 40; Jerónimo de Mendieta, *Historia
eclesiástica indiana* (Mexico: Porrúa, 1971), vol. 1, ch. 5, p.
29.

34. Gomes, *A filosofia arabigo-portuguesa*, pp. 3, 15.

35. Diogo Velho da Chancelaria, in G. de Resende, *Cancioneiro
geral* (Gomes, *A filosofia arabigo-portuguesa*, p. 323);
Tomaz and Alves, 'Da cruzada ao quinto império', pp.
91–2, 126.

36. Milhou, 'La tentación joaquinita en los principios de la
Compañía de Jesús', p. 206. The Society of Jesus had originally intended to convert the Muslims of the Holy Land,
but the first fathers went to India.

37. Milhou, *Colomb et le messianisme hispanique*, pp. 320–1.

38. J. Garcia Oro, *El cardenal Cisneros. Vida y empresas*, vol.
2 (Madrid: 1993), BAC, vol. 528, pp. 537–90.

39. Alba, *Acerca de algunas particularidades de las comunidades de Castilla*, p. 173.

40. '[Los Moros] non sabrán de sí que se fazer ni que consejo
tomar sino que desearán mucho estar en el rreyno de
aliemde, y ajuntarse an para el agua pasar y tanta será la
gente de los moros agarenos que en los nabios entrarán que
los navios con ellos se fundirán, y más de la tercia parte
dellos morirán a espada y la otra terçia parte uiran . . .':
ibid., p. 191.

41. Bandarra was condemned in Lisbon in 1541.

42. 'Carta ao padre André Fernandes', 29 April 1659, in
António Vieira, *Cartas*, ed. João Lúcio de Azevedo, vol. 1
(Coimbra: Imprensa da Universidade, 1925), pp. 484–6.

43. Ibid., pp. 484–5.

44. Milhou, 'La tentación joaquinita en los principios de la
Compañía de Jesús', p. 196.

45. As is well known, Sebastian died without an heir and Philip
II seized the Portuguese Crown, achieving in his own person
the union of the two empires.

46. Before his *Discurso da vida do sempre bem vindo e appare-
cido Don Sebastião*, published in Paris in 1602, João de
Castro had written *Da quinta e última monarquia futura
con muitas outras coisas admiravéis dos nossos tempos*

(Paris: 1597). Nor was it a matter simply of dreams or airy-fairy ideas. João de Castro supported the claims of a false Sebastian, Marco Tulio Catizone, a Calabrian ex-hermit who appeared in Venice, where he lived for some time surrounded by Portuguese exiles.

47. Henrico Martínez, *Repertorio de los tiempos* (Mexico: Secretaría de Educación Pública, 1958), p. 268.
48. Gomes, *A filosofia arabigo-portuguesa*, p. 325.
49. Islamic messianism – western Islamism in the form of Mahdism – was closely related to Jewish and Christian messianisms: Gomes, *A filosofia arabigo-portuguesa*, p. 324.
50. Harvey, *Muslims in Spain*, p. 230.
51. Ibid., pp. 295–6.
52. The English adventurer Robert Sherley proposed to Spain that they make a deal with the Turks so as to be able to destroy as a priority the Protestant heresy: see *Peso Politico do Todo el Mundo d'Anthony Sherley, ou un aventurier anglais au service de l'Espagne*, ed. Xavier-A. Flores (Paris: SEVPEN, 1963).
53. Martínez, *Repertorio*, p. 231.
54. Alain Milhou, 'De la destruction de l'Espagne à la destruction des Indes (Notes sur l'emploi des termes *destroyr, destruymiento, destruición, destroydor* de la Primera Crónica General a Las Casas)', *Mélanges à la mémoire d'André Joucla-Ruau* (Aix-en-Provence: Université de Provence, 1978), pp. 907–19.
55. Milhou, 'De la destruction de l'Espagne à la destruction des Indes', *Etudes sur l'impact culturel du Nouveau Monde*, vol. 1, p. 29.
56. Ibid., p. 46.
57. For example, Sancho de Moncada, author of a *Restauración política de España* [1619], ed. Jean Vilar (Madrid: Instituto de Estudios fiscales, 1974).
58. Martínez, *Repertorio*, p. 227.

8 Islam in the New World

1. Sylviane A. Diouf, *Servants of Allah: African Muslims Enslaved in the Americas* (New York–London: New York University Press, 1998).

2. Nabil Matar, *Turks, Moors and Englishmen in the Age of Discovery* (New York: Columbia University Press, 1999), p. 9.

3. Woodrow Borah, *Silk Raising in Colonial Mexico* (Los Angeles: University of California Press, 1943), p. 9.

4. For a Morisco from the Alpujarras who had remained Muslim, see José Toribio Medina, *Historia del tribunal del Santo Oficio de la Inquisición en México* (Mexico: Ediciones Fuente Cultural, 1952), p. 134.

5. Matar, *Turks, Moors and Englishmen*, p. 100.

6. Laura de Mello e Souza, *O diabo e a terra de Santa Cruz* (São Paulo: Companhia das Letras, 1987), pp. 216–26 (trans. as *The Devil and the Land of the Holy Cross: Witchcraft, Slavery, and Popular Religion in Colonial Brazil* (Austin: University of Texas Press, 2003); João José Reis, *Rebelião escrava no Brasil* (São Paulo: Companhia das Letras, 2003), p. 159 (trans. Arthur Brakel as *Slave Rebellion in Brazil: the Muslim Uprising of 1835 in Bahia* (Baltimore: Johns Hopkins University Press, 1995).

7. Louis Cardaillac, *Morisques et chrétiens. Un affrontement polémique (1492–1640)* (Paris: Klincksieck, 1977).

8. Rafael López Guzmán, Lázaro Gila Medina, Ignacio Henares Cuellas and Guillermo Tovar de Teresa, *Arquitectura y carpintería mudejar en Nueva España* (Mexico: Azabache, 1992); Cynthia Robinson, 'Mudejar revisited. A prolegoména to the reconstruction of perception, devotion and experience at the Mudéjar convent of Clarisas, Tordesillas, Spain (fourteenth century A.D.)', *Res*, 43 (Spring, 2003), pp. 51–77; Jeanette Favrot Peterson, *The Paradise Garden Murals of Malinalco. Utopia and Empire in Sixteenth-Century Mexico* (Austin: University of Texas Press, 1993).

9. Louis Cardaillac, 'Le problème morisque en Amérique', *Mélanges de la Casa de Velasquez*, 12 (1976), pp. 283–306; Antonio Garrido Aranda, *Moriscos e Indios* (Mexico: Universidad nacional autónoma de México, 1980).

10. For the role of the Spanish chronicles devoted to North Africa, in many respects very similar to those of the Indies, see Mercedes García-Arenal in her introduction to the work of Diego de Torres, *Historia de los Xarifes* (Madrid: Siglo XXI, 1980); Miguel Angel A. de Bulnes, *La imagen de los musulmanes y del norte de Africa en la España de los siglos*

XVI y XVII (Madrid: Centro superior de investigaciones científicas, 1989); Miguel Angel A. de Bulnes, 'El descubrimiento de América y la conquista del Norte de Africa, dos empresas paralelas en la Edad Modena', *Revista de Indias*, 45 (1985), pp. 225–33. The comparisons with the Muslim populations applied equally for the distant populations of Asia; for Juan González de Mendoza, the Chinese of Canton were '*morenos como los de Fez o Berberia*': *Historia del gran reino de la China* (Rome: 1585).

11. Alexandra Merle, *Le Miroir ottoman. Une image politique des hommes dans la littérature géographique espagnole et française (XVIe-XVIIe siècle)* (Paris: Presses de l'Université de Paris-Sorbonne, 2003), p. 104.

12. *Le Voyage et itinéraire de oultre mer faict par frere Jehan Thenaud*, ed. C. Schefer (Paris: E. Leroux, 1884), ch. 2, pp. 46–8.

13. Hernán Cortés, *Cartas y documentos*, ed. Mario Hernández Sánchez-Barba (Mexico: Porrúa, 1963), pp. 45, 51, 73.

14. Luis Weckmann, *La herencia medieval de México* (Mexico: Fondo de cultura económica, 1984), vol. 1, p. 145; Gonzalo Fernández de Oviedo, *Historia general y natural de las Indias* (Madrid: 1851–5), vol. 4, pp. 220–1.

15. Weckmann, *La herencia medieval de México*, vol. 1, p. 145. The Arabs were also compared to the Indians because of their brown colour: Merle, *Le Miroir ottoman*, p. 143.

16. Matar, *Turks, Moors and Englishmen*, pp. 98–9.

17. For example, the reference to '*mamelucos e cafuzos*' slaves working in sugar plantations in November 1725 (Archivo Histórico Ultramarino, Lisbon, ACL CU 013, Cx.9, D.786), or a demand for a 'tapuia or mameluca' slave in May 1727 (ibid., Cx.10, D.909).

18. Andrew Wheatcroft, *Infidels. A History of the Conflict between Christendom and Islam* (London: Viking, 2003), p. 123.

19. J. T. Johnson and John Kelsey (eds), *Cross, Crescent and Sword* (New York: Greenwood, 1990), in Wheatcroft, *Infidels*, p. 396; J. T. Johnson, *The Holy War Idea in Western and Islamic Traditions* (University Park, Pa: Pennsylvania State University Press, 1997).

20. Wheatcroft, *Infidels*, p. 199; see also R. A. Fletcher, *Saint James's Catapult: the Life and Times of Diego Gelmírez of*

Santiago de Compostella (Oxford: Oxford University Press, 1984).

21. Teresa Gisbert, *Iconografia e mitos indígenas en el arte* (La Paz: Ed. Gisbert and Cia, 1980), pp. 197–8; Irene Silverblatt, 'Political memories and colonizing symbols: Santiago and the mountain gods of colonial Peru', in Jonathan D. Hill, *Rethinking History and Myth. Indigenous South American Perspectives on the Past* (Urbana: University of Illinois Press, 1988), pp. 174–94.

22. Max Harris, *Aztecs, Moors and Christians. Festivals of Reconquest in Mexico and Spain* (Austin: University of Texas Press, 2000), p. 118.

23. Toribio Benavente Motolinía, *Memoriales*, ed. Edmundo O'Gorman (Mexico: Universidad nacional autónoma de México, 1971), pp. 106–13; Delno C. West, 'Medieval ideas of apocalyptic mission and the early Franciscans in Mexico', *The Americas*, XCLV, 3 (January 1989), pp. 293–313.

24. The Jerusalem of the sixteenth century, pitiful and sad, was much less interesting to travellers and pilgrims than the Jerusalem of the time of Christ: see Merle, *Le Miroir ottoman*, p. 110, quoting Antonio de Lisboa and Diego de Mérida.

25. Nicolás Rangel, *Historia del toreo en México* (Mexico: Editorial Cosmos, 1980), p. 34.

26. Alfonso Alfaro, *Moros y cristianos. Una batalla cósmica* (Mexico: Artes de México, Consejo nacional para las artes, 2001).

27. Motolinía, *Memoriales*, p. 106.

28. Barbara Fuchs, *Mimesis and Empire. The New World, Islam and European Identities* (Cambridge: Cambridge University Press, 2001), pp. 74–5.

29. This is how Mendieta interpreted Book 4 of Esdras. García (1607) was of the same opinion.

30. Ramón Alba, *Acerca de algunas particularidades de las comunidades de Castilla* (Madrid: Editorial Nacional, 1975), p. 205.

31. *Monumenta mexicana*, ed. Felix Zubillaga (Rome: Institutum Societatis Jesus), vol. 1, doc. 62, pp. 142–3.

32. Fernan González de Eslava, 'Colóquio de la batalla naval que el sereníssimo príncipe Don Juan de Austria tuvo con el Turco', *Coloquios espirituales y sacramentales*, ed. Othón Arróniz

Báez (Mexico: El Colegio de México, 1998), p. 495 ('Mahoma, toi vouloir que chrétiens me vaincre moi?/Pourquoi pas venir à mon aide?/ Pourquoi promesse pas tenir?/ Pourquoi dire? Moi faire mes dévotions à la mosquée . . . /maintenant perdre Torquie me fendre le coeur.')

33. Motolinía, *Memoriales*, p. 157.
34. Vidal Abril Castelló, *Francisco de la Cruz, Inquisición, Actas I & II* (Madrid: Centro superior de investigaciones científicas, 1992–6).
35. Davide Bigalli, *Millenarismo e America* (Milan: Cortina, 2000); Frank Graziano, *The Millennial New World* (New York–Oxford: Oxford University Press, 1999).
36. Serge Gruzinski, *Les Hommes-Dieux du Mexique* (Paris: Editions des Archives contemporaines, 1985); Graziano, *The Millennial New World*.
37. For the Iberian triangulation, see the suggestive ideas of Fuchs (*Mimesis and Empire*).
38. Matar, *Turks, Moors and Englishmen*, p. 130, quoting Joseph Mead (1586–1638).
39. Ibid., p. 133.
40. One thinks of Daniel Defoe and his *A Plan of the English Commerce*; see Matar, *Turks, Moors and Englishmen*, pp. 170–2.

9 Thinking the World

1. In the sense of the Heideggerian *Weltbild*: Martin Heidegger, *Chemins qui ne mènent nulle part* (Paris: Gallimard, 2006), p. 116, English trans. *Pathmarks*, ed. William McNeill (Cambridge: Cambridge University Press, 1998).
2. Published in 1591, the *Relazioni universali* was frequently republished and translated and influential in both Catholic and Protestant territories.
3. Giovanni Botero, *Relazioni universali* (Brescia: 1599), Prima parte, p. 270; see also Maria Matilde Benzoni, ' "L'apertura del mondo", Pierre Martyr d'Anghiera et les réseaux d'information sur le Mexique, l'Amérique espagnole et le Monde dans l'Italie du XVIe siècle', unpublished doctoral thesis, Paris, EHESS, 2006, p. 333.
4. In the fifth and final part of the *Relationi universali*.

5. Tommaso Campanella, *Monarchie d'Espagne et monarchie de France*, ed. Germana Ernst (Paris: PUF, 1997), pp. 27, 206, 321.

6. Ibid., p. 317. Africa was quickly dispatched, Persia was of interest as a potential ally against the Turks, Cathay was put aside 'because it is not on the shipping lane to Spain'. See Noel Malcolm, 'The Crescent and the City of the Sun: Islam and the Renaissance Utopia of Tommaso Campanella', *Proceedings of the British Academy*, 125 (2004), pp. 41–67.

7. Campanella, *Monarchie d'Espagne*, p. 339.

8. 'Ralegh's importance is that he employed a secular and critical approach to a study of world history which was in a very large part a study of Biblical history; and that he did it in English in a work which was a bestseller': Christopher Hill, *Intellectual Origins of the English Revolution Revisited* (Oxford: Clarendon Press, 1997), p. 168.

9. William O. Beeman, *The 'Great Satan' versus the 'Mad Mullahs'. How the United States and Iran Demonize Each Other* (Westport: Praeger, 2005).

10. Luis Felipe F. Tomaz and Jorge Santos Alves, 'Da cruzada ao quinto império', *A Memoria da nação* (Lisbon: Sá da Costa Editoria, 1991), p. 138.

11. Campanella, *Monarchie d'Espagne*, p. 47.

12. For the 'Turkish obsession' in the long term, in mental worlds as well as in daily life, see Giovanni Ricci, *Ossessione turca. In una retrovia cristiana dell'Europa moderna* (Bologna: Il Mulino, 2002).

13. Alain Milhou, 'La tentación joaquinita en los principios de la Compañía de Jesús. El caso de Francisco Borja y Andrés de Oviedo', *Florensia, Bollettino del Centro Internazionale di Studi Gioachimiti*, year VIII–IX (1994–5), pp. 193–239.

14. The imprecations of Zain al-Dîn Ma'bari, who preached *djihad* in the Indian Ocean, bear little relation to the reality of dealings between Portuguese and Muslims.

15. Hill, *Intellectual Origins of the English Revolution Revisited*, p. 144; Sir Walter Ralegh, *History of the World*, vol. 6 (Edinburgh: Archibald Constable and Co., 1820), p. 369.

16. Hill, *Intellectual Origins of the English Revolution Revisited*, p. 143; Ralegh, *History of the World*, vol. 2, pp. 91–2.

17. Campanella, *Monarchie d'Espagne*, pp. 53, 35.

18. See Sanjay Subrahmanyam, 'On world historians in the sixteenth century', *Representations*, 91 (2005), p. 32. At the

other end of Asia, the Chinese imperial court hoped that the scientific knowledge of the Jesuits would provide firmer foundations for the astrological predictions which guaranteed the supremacy of the emperor.

19. Henrico Martínez, *Repertorio de los tiempos* (Mexico: Secretaría de Educación Pública, 1958), p. 215; Campanella composed on this occasion the *Pronostico astrologico* which became the last chapter of the *larticuli prophetales'*. See T. Campanella, *Opusculi astrologici: Come evitare il Fato Astrale, Apologetico, Disputa sulla Bolle*, ed. Germana Ernst (Milan: 2003), p. 11.

20. Campanella, *Monarchie d'Espagne*, p. 27 and note 42.

21. And more than 14 million for 'messiah', on the same date.

22. See Antonio de Leon Pinelo, *El paraiso en el nuevo mundo* [1650], prologue Raúl Porras Barrenechea, Comité del IV Centenario del descubrimiento del Amazonas (Lima: 1943); Antonio de Santa Maria Jaboatão, *Orbe seráfico novo brasileiro* [Lisbon: 1761] (Rio de Janeiro: Instituto Histórico e Geográfico Brasileiro, 1856–62).

23. Serge Gruzinski, 'Von *Matrix* zu Campanella. Kulturelle Métissagen und Mondialisierungen', in Jens Badura (ed.), *Mondialisierungen. 'Globalisierung' in Lichte tranzdisziplinärer Reflexionen* (Bielefeld: Transcript Verlag, 2006), pp. 103–22.

24. Peter Sloterdijk, *Esferas II. Globos. Macrosferologia* (Madrid: Siruela, 2004), p. 854.

25. *Voyageurs arabes, Ibn Fadlan, Ibn Jubayr, Ibn Battuta*, Collection 'Bibliothèque de La Pléiade' (Paris: Gallimard, 1995).

26. Campanella, *Monarchie d'Espagne*, p. 361.

Conclusion: What Time is it There?

1. Bartolomé and Lucile Bennassar, *Les Chrétiens d'Allah. L'histoire extraordinaire des renégats, XVIe–XVIIe siècle* (Paris: Perrin, 1989).

2. For Cervantes and the Turks, see Ottmar Hegyi, *Cervantes and the Turks: Historical Reality Versus Literary Fiction in 'La Gran Sultana' and 'El amante liberal'* (Newark, Delaware: Juan de la Cuesta, 1992)

Bibliography

Abboud, Soha, 'Apocalipsis, resurrección y Juicio Final en la cultura islámica', in Adeline Rucquoi et al., *En pos del tercer milenio. Apocalíptica, mesianismo, milenarismo e historia* (Salamanca: Ediciones Universidad, 2000), pp. 43–77.

Abril Castelló, Vidal, *Francisco de la Cruz, Inquisición, Actas I & II* (Madrid: Centro superior de investigaciones científicas, 1992–6).

Acosta, José de, *Historia natural y moral de las Indias*, ed. Edmundo O'Gorman (Mexico: Fondo de cultura económica, 1979), trans. Frances Lopez-Morillas, ed. Jane E. Mangan, as *The Natural and Moral History of the Indies* (Durham, NC–London: Duke University Press, 2002).

Alam, Muzaffar and Sanjay Subrahmanyam (eds), *The Mughal State, 1526–1750* (Delhi-Oxford: Oxford University Press, 1998).

Alfaro, Alfonso, *Moros y cristianos. Una batalla cósmica* (Mexico: Artes de México, Consejo nacional para las artes, 2001).

Atkinson, Geoffroy, *Les Nouveaux Horizons de la Renaissance française* (Paris: Droz, 1935).

Aubin, Jean, *Le Latin et l'Astrolabe: recherches sur le Portugal de la Renaissance, son expansion en Asie et les relations internationales*, 2 vols (Paris: Centre culturel Calouste Gulbenkian, 1996–2000).

Balbuena, Bernardo de, *La grandeza mexicana y compendio apologético en alabanza de la poesía*, ed. Luis Adolfo Domínguez (Mexico: Editorial Porrúa, 1990).

Bataillon, Marcel, *Erasmo y España, Estudios sobre la historia espiritual del siglo XVI* (Mexico: Fondo de cultura económica, 1982).

Bennassar, Bartolomé and Lucile Bennassar, *Les Chrétiens d'Allah. L'histoire extraordinaire des renégats, XVIe–XVIIe siècle* (Paris: Perrin, 1989).

Bernard, Carmen, *Un Inca platonicien, Garcilaso de la Vega* (Paris: Fayard, 2006).

Bigalli, Davide, *Millenarismo e America* (Milan: Cortina, 2000).

Binding, Paul, *Imagined Corners: Exploring the World's First Atlas* (London: Headlines Books, 2003).

Braudel, Fernand, *La Mediterranée et le monde mediterranéen à l'époque de Philippe II* (Paris: Armand Colin, 1990), trans. Siân Reynolds as *The Mediterranean and the Mediterranean World in the Age of Philip II*, 2 vols (London: Collins, 1972–3; repr. Fontana, 1975).

Broc, Numa, *La Géographie de la Renaissance (1420–1620)* (Paris: Bibliothèque nationale, 1986), trans. Italian as *La geografia del Rinascimento, Cosmografi, geografi, viaggiatori, 1420–1620* (Modena: Panini Franco Cosimo, 1996).

Brotton, Jerry, *Trading Territories. Mapping the Early Modern World* (London: Reaktion Books, 1997).

Brummett, Palmira, *Ottoman Seapower and Levantine Diplomacy in the Age of Discovery* (Albany: Suny Press, 1994).

Bulnes, Miguel Angel de, *La imagen de los musulmanes y del norte de Africa en la España de los siglos XVI y XVII: los carácteres de una hostilidad* (Madrid: Centro superior de investigaciones científicas, 1989).

Campanella, Tommaso, *Monarchie d'Espagne et monarchie de France*, ed. Germana Ernst (Paris: PUF, 1997).

Campanella, Tommaso, *Opusculi astrologici: Come evitare il Fato Astrale, Apologetico, Disputa sulle Bolle*, ed. Germana Ernst (Milan: 2003).

Cañizares-Esguerra, Jorge, *Nature, Empire and Nation. Explorations of the History of Science in the Iberian World* (Stanford: Stanford University Press, 2006).

Cantimori, Delio, *Eretici italiani del Cinquecento* (Turin: Einaudi, 2002).

Cardaillac, Louis, *Morisques et chrétiens. Un affrontement polémique (1492–1640)* (Paris: Klincksieck, 1977).

Casale, Gian Carlo, 'The Ottoman Age of Exploration: Spices, Maps and Conquest in the Sixteenth Century Indian Ocean', unpublished Ph. D. thesis, Harvard University, 2004.

Casale, Gian Carlo, 'A Caliph, a Canal and Twenty Thousand Cannibals: Global Politics in the 1580s' (*www.usc.edu/schools/college/crcc/private/ierc/Caliph_Canal_Cannibals.pdf*).

Cieza de León, Pedro, *Primera parte de la cronica del Perú que trata de la demarcación de sus provincias, la descripción dellas, las fundaciones de las nuevas ciudades, los ritos y costumbres de los Indios, con otras cosas dignas de saberse* (Seville: 1553) (Italian trans., Rome: 1555).

Clavijo, Ruy González de, *Embajada a Tamerlán*, ed. Francisco López Estrada (Madrid: Editorial Castalia, 2004).

Cordano, Federica, *La Geografia degli antichi* (Bari: Laterza, 2006).

Couto, Diogo do, *Diogo do Couto e a década 8a da Asia*, ed. Maria Augusta Lima Cruz, Comissão Nacional para as Comemorações dos Descobrimentos (Lisbon: Imprensa Nacional, 1994).

Couto, Diogo do, *O soldado prático*, ed. Reis Brasil, Mem Martins (Lisbon: Publicações Europa-América, 1988).

Diouf, Sylviane A., *Servants of Allah: African Muslims Enslaved in the Americas* (New York–London: New York University Press, 1998).

Dodds, Jerrilynn D., Thomas F. Glick and Vivian B. Man (eds), *Convivencia: Jews, Muslims and Christians in Medieval Spain* (New York: G. Braziller, 1992).

Fernández del Castillo, Francisco, *Libros y libreros en el siglo XVI* (Mexico: Fondo de cultura económica, 1982).

Fleisher, 'Royal authority, dynastic cyclism and "Ibn Khaldunism" in sixteenth century Ottoman letters', *Journal of Asian and African Studies*, 18, 3–4 (1983), pp. 198–220.

Fuchs, Barbara, *Mimesis and Empire. The New World, Islam and European Identities* (Cambridge: Cambridge University Press, 2001).

Galvão, Antônio, *Tratado dos descobrimentos* [Lisbon: 1563] (Barcelos: Livraria Civilização Editoria, 1987).

Garin, Eugenio, *La cultura filosofica del Rinascimento italiano. Ricerche e documenti* (Florence: Sansoni, 1961; Milan: Bompiani, 2001).

Gisbert, Teresa, *Iconografía e mitos indígenas en el arte* (La Paz: Ed. Gisbert and Cia, 1980).

Goffman, Daniel, *The Ottoman Empire and Early Modern Europe* (Cambridge: Cambridge University Press, 2002).

Gomes, Pinharanda, *A história da filosofia portuguesa*, vol. 3: *A filosofia arabigo-portuguesa* (Lisbon: Guimarães Editores, 1991).

González de Eslava, Fernan, *Coloquios espirituales y sacramentales*, ed. Othón Arróniz Báez (Mexico: El Colegio de México, 1998).

González Sánchez, Carlos Alberto, *Los mundos del libro. Medios de difusión de la cultura occidental en las Indias del los siglos XVI y XVII* (Seville: University of Seville, 2001).

Goodrich, Thomas D., *The Ottoman Turks and the New World. A Study of Tarih-i Hind-i garbi and Sixteenth Century Ottoman America* (Wiesbaden: Otto Harrassowitz, 1990).

Grafton, Anthony, *Cardano's Cosmos: the World and Works of a Renaissance Astrologer* (Cambridge, Mass.: Harvard University Press, 2000).

Graziano, Frank, *The Millennial New World* (New York–Oxford: Oxford University Press, 1999).

Greenleaf, Richard E., *La Inquisición en Nueva España. Siglo XVI* (Mexico: Fondo de cultura económica, 1981).

Gruzinski, Serge, *Les Quatre Parties du monde. Histoire d'une mondialisation* (Paris: La Martinière, 2004).

Hamdani, Abbas, 'Columbus and the recovery of Jerusalem', *Journal of the American Oriental Society*, 99, 1 (January–March 1979), pp. 39–48.

Hamdani, Abbas, 'Ottoman response to the discovery of America and the new route to India', *Journal of the American Oriental Society*, 101, 3 (July–September 1981), pp. 323–30.

Harris, Max, *Aztecs, Moors and Christians. Festivals of Reconquest in Mexico and Spain* (Austin: University of Texas Press, 2000).

Harvey, L. P., *Muslims in Spain, 1500 to 1614* (Chicago–London: Chicago University Press, 2005).

Herrera y Tordesillas, Antonio de, *Historia general de los hechos de los Castellanos en las islas i tierra firme del mar oceano*, 7 vols (Madrid: Emprenta Real, 1601–15).

Hess, Andrew C., 'Piri Reis and the Ottoman response to the voyages of discovery', *Terrae Incognitae*, 6 (1974), pp. 19–37.

Hill, Christopher, *Intellectual Origins of the English Revolution Revisited* (Oxford: Clarendon Press, 1997).

Hungaria, Georgius of, *Des turcs: traité sur les moeurs, les coutumes et la perfidie des Turcs*, trans. and ed. Joel Schnapp (Toulouse: Anacharsis, 2007).

Idrîsî, *La Première Géographie de l'Occident*, ed. François Bresc and Annliese Neff (Paris: GF-Flammarion, 1989).

Inalcik, Halil, *An Economic and Social History of the Ottoman Empire* (Cambridge: Cambridge University Press, 1997).

Israël, Jonathan I., *Diasporas Within a Diaspora, Jews, Crypto-Jews and the World Maritime Empires (1540–1740)* (Leiden: Brill, 2002).

Jardine, Lisa and Jerry Brotton, *Global Interests. Renaissance Art between East and West* (London: Reaktion Books, 2000).

Kafadar, Cemal, 'The Ottomans and Europe', in Thomas Brady Jr, Heiko A. Oberman and James D. Tracy (eds) *Handbook of European History, 1400–1600: Later Middle Ages. Renaissance and Reformation*, vol. 1 (Leiden: Brill, 1994), pp. 589–635.

Kagan, Richard L., *Lucrecia's Dreams: Politics and Prophecy in Sixteenth-Century Spain* (Berkeley: University of California Press, 1990).

King, Willard F., *Juan Ruiz de Alarcón, letrado y dramaturgo. Su mundo mexicano y español* (Mexico: El Colegio de México, 1989).

Lewis, Bernard, *Islam and the West* (Oxford: Oxford University Press, 1993).

Lewis, Bernard, *The Muslim Discovery of Europe* (London–New York: W. W. Norton & Company, 1982, 2001).

Llaguno, J., *La Personalidad jurídica del indio y el II Concilio Provincial Mexicano* [1585] (Mexico: Porrúa, 1963).

McIntosh, Gregory, *The Piri Reis Map of 1513* (Athens–London: University of Georgia Press, 2000).

Malcolm, Noel, 'The Crescent and the City of the Sun: Islam and the Renaissance Utopia of Tommaso Campanella', *Proceedings of the British Academy*, 125 (2004), pp. 41–67.

Mantran, Robert (ed.) *Histoire de l'Empire ottoman* (Paris: Fayard, 1989).

Martínez, Henrico, *Repertorio de los tiempos*, ed. Francisco de La Maza (Mexico: Secretaría de Educación Pública, 1958).

Mas, Albert, *Les Turcs dans la littérature espagnole du Siècle d'or: recherches sur l'évolution d'un thème littéraire*, 2 vols (Paris: Centre de recherches hispaniques, 1967).

Matar, Nabil, *Turks, Moors and Englishmen in the Age of Discovery* (New York: Columbia University Press, 1999).

Mathes, Valerie R., 'Enrico Martínez of New Spain', *Americas*, 33, 1 (July 1976), pp. 62–77.

Maza, Francisco de la, *Enrico Martínez, cosmografo e impresor de Nueva España* (Mexico: Secretaría de Educación Pública, 1943; Universidad nacional autónoma de México, 1991).

Medina, José Toribio, *La Imprenta en México (1539–1821)* (Mexico: Universidad nacional autónoma de México, 1989).

Merle, Alexandra, *Le Miroir ottoman. Une image politique des hommes dans la littérature géographique espagnole et française (XVIe–XVIIe siècle)* (Paris: Presses de l'Université de Paris-Sorbonne, 2003).

Milhou, Alain, 'De la destruction de l'Espagne à la destruction des Indes: histoire sacrée et combats idéologiques', *Etudes sur l'impact culturel du Nouveau Monde*, vol. 1, pp. 25–47, vol. 3, pp. 11–54 (Paris: L'Harmattan, 1981–3).

Milhou, Alain, *Colón y su mentalidad mesiánica en el ambiente franciscanista español* (Valladolid: 1983), trans. French as *Colomb et le messianisme hispanique* (Gap: Presses universitaires de la Méditerranée, 2007).

Milhou, Alain, 'La tentación joaquinita en los principios de la Compañía de Jesús. El caso de Francisco Borja y Andrés de Oviedo', *Florensia, Bollettino del Centro Internazionale di Studi Gioachimiti*, year VIII–IX (1994–5) pp. 193–239.

Miquel, André, *L'Islam et sa civilisation, VIIe–XXe siècle* (Paris: Armand Colin, 1977).

Moreno Corral, Marco A., 'La *Physica speculatio*, primer libro de física escrito y publicado en el continente americano', *Revista mexicana de física*, 50, 1 (2004), pp. 74–80.

Morga, Antonio de, *Sucesos de las islas Filipinas* [Mexico: 1609] (Madrid: Polífemo, 1997).

Mota y Escobar, Alonsa de la, *Descripción geográfica de los reinos de Nueva Galicia, Nueva León y Nueva Viscaya* (Mexico: Pedro Robredo, 1940).

Motolinía, Toribio Benavente, *Memoriales*, ed. Edmundo O'Gorman (Mexico: Universidad nacional autónoma de México, 1971).

Parker, Geoffrey, 'David or Goliath? Philip II and his World in the 1580s', in Geoffrey Parker and Richard L. Kagan (eds), *Spain, Europe and the Atlantic World. Essays in Honour of John H. Elliott* (Cambridge: Cambridge University Press, 1995).

Parker, Geoffrey, *The World is not Enough. The Grand Strategy of Philip II* (New Haven: Yale University Press, 1998).

Perez, Joseph, *Isabelle et Ferdinand, rois catholiques d'Espagne* (Paris: Fayard, 1998).

Pertusi, Agostino, *Fine di Bisanzio e fine del mondo. Significato e ruolo storico delle profezie sulla caduta di Costantinopoli in Oriente e Occidente*, ed. E. Morini (Rome: Istituto Storico per il Medio Evo, 1988).

Phelan, John Leddy, *The Millenial Kingdom of the Franciscans in the New World* (Berkeley: University of California Press, 1970).

Polybe, *Histoire*, ed. François Hartog (Paris: Gallimard, 2003).

Prosperi, Adriano, *America e apocalisse et altri saggi* (Pisa–Rome: Istituto Editoriali Poligrafici Internazionali, 1999).

Rahman Farooqi, Naimur, *Mughal–Ottoman Relations: a Study of Political and Diplomatic Relations Between Mughal India and the Ottoman Empire, 1556–1749* (Delhi: Idarah-i Adabiyat-i Delli, 1989).

Ramusio, Giovanni Battista, *Navigationi et Viaggi*, I (Venice: Tommaso Giunti, 1563).

Rangel, Nicolás, *Historia del toreo en México* (Mexico: Editorial Cosmos, 1980).

Reeves, Marjorie, *The Influence of Prophecy in the Later Middle Ages* (Oxford: Clarendon Press, 1969).

Reis, João José, *Rebelião escrava no Brasil* (São Paulo: Companhia das Letras, 2003).

Ricci, Giovanni, *Ossessione turca. In una retrovia cristiana dell'Europa moderna* (Bologna: Il Mulino, 2002).

Robinson, Cynthia, 'Mudejar revisited. A prolegoména to the reconstruction of perception, devotion and experience at the Mudéjar convent of Clarisas, Tordesillas, Spain (fourteenth century A.D.)' *Res*, 43 (Spring, 2003), pp. 51–77.

Rodríguez-Sala, María Luisa, *El eclipse de luna. Misión científica de Felipe II en Nueva España* (Huelva: Biblioteca Montaniana, Universidad de Huelva, 1998).

Rodríguez-Sala, María Luisa, *Letrados y técnicos de los siglos XVI y XVII* (Mexico: Universidad nacional autónoma de México & Miguel Angel Porrúa, 2002).

Rubiés, Joan-Pau, *Travel and Ethnology in the Renaissance: South India Through European Eyes, 1250–1625* (Cambridge: Cambridge University Press, 2000).

Sandoval, Fray Prudencio de, *Historia de la vida y hechos del emperador Carlos V máximo, fortísmo, Rey Católico de España y de las Indias, Islas y Tierra firme del mar Océano*, ed. Carlos Seco Serrano, 3 vols, (Madrid: Atlas, 1955–6) (Biblioteca de autores españoles, vols 80–2).

Sansovino, Francesco, *Historia Universale dell'Origine, Guerre et Imperio de Turchi* (Venice: 1564).

Schell Hoberman, Luisa, 'Enrico Martínez, printer and engineer', in David Sweet and Gary Nash (eds), *Struggle and Survival* (Berkeley: University of California Press, 1981).

Schmidt, Benjamin, *Beyond Innocence. The Dutch Imagination and the New World, 1570–1670* (Cambridge: Cambridge University Press, 2002).

Seyyidi 'Ali Reis, *The Travels and Adventures of the Turkish Admiral Sidi Ali Reïs in India, Afghanistan, Central Asia and Persia During the Years 1553–1556* (London: 1899).

Sloterdijk, Peter, *Esferas II. Globos. Macrosferologia* (Madrid: Siruela, 2004) (originally published Frankfurt-am-Main: Suhrkamp Verlag, 1999).

Stars and the End of the World in Luther's Time, ed. Paola Zembelli (Berlin–New York: W. de Gruyter, 1986).

Subrahmanyam, Sanjay, 'On world historians in the sixteenth century', *Representations*, 91 (2005), pp. 26–57.

Subrahmanyam, Sanjay, 'Taking stock of the Franks: South Asian views of Europeans and Europe, 1500–1800', *The Indian Economic and Social History Review* (New Delhi), 42, 1 (2005), pp. 69–100.

Thornton, William, *New World Empire: Civil Islam, Terrorism and the Making of Neoglobalism* (Lanham, Md: Rowman and Littlefield, 2005).

Tomaz, Luis Felipe F. and Jorge Santos Alves, 'Da cruzada ao quinto império', in *A Memoria da nação* (Lisbon: Sá da Costa Editoria, 1991), pp. 81–165.

Vitoria, Francisco de, *Relectio de Indis. La questione degli Indios*, ed. A. Lamacchia (Bari: Levante Editori, 1996).

Vitoria, Francisco de, *De jure belli*, ed. Carlo Galli (Bari: Laterza, 2005).

Vivero, Rodrigo de, *Du Japon et du bon gouvernement de l'Espagne et des Indes*, ed. Juliette Montbeig (Paris: SEVPEN, 1972).

Voyageurs arabes, Ibn Fadlan, Ibn Jubayr, Ibn Battuta, Collection 'Bibliothèque de La Pléiade' (Paris: Gallimard, 1995).

Weckmann, Luis, *La herencia medieval de México*, 2 vols (Mexico: Fondo de cultura económica, 1984).

Wheatcroft, Andrew, *Infidels. A History of the Conflict between Christendom and Islam* (London: Penguin Books, 2004).

Yerasimos, Stephane, *La Fondation de Constantinople et de Sainte-Sophie dans les traditions turques* (Istanbul–Paris: Iletisim Yayinlari, 1990).

Index